SNOOPY'S
Guide *to the* Writing Life

Edited by Barnaby Conrad
and Monte Schulz

WRITER'S DIGEST BOOKS
Cincinnati, Ohio
www.writersdigest.com

Jack Canfield's piece is reprinted with permission from the author. It originally appeared in *Chicken Soup for the Writer's Soul*.

Sections of the introduction by Barnaby Conrad reprinted by permission of The New York Times Co. ©1967.

Dominick Dunne's piece is reprinted with permission from the author. It originally appeared in *The Complete Guide to Fiction Writing*.

Oakley Hall's piece is reprinted with permission from Writer's Digest Books and the author. It originally appeared in *The Art & Craft of Novel Writing*.

John Leggett's piece is reprinted with permission from the author. It originally appeared in *The Complete Guide to Fiction Writing*.

Budd Schulberg's piece is reprinted with permission from the author. It originally appeared in *Love, Action, Laughter*.

Danielle Steel's piece is reprinted with permission from the author. It originally appeared in *The Complete Guide to Fiction Writing*.

Sol Stein's piece is reprinted by permission of St. Martin's Press, LLC. Copyright © 2000 by Sol Stein. It originally appeared in *Stein on Writing* by Sol Stein.

Peanuts ® Comic Strips: © United Feature Syndicate, Inc. All comic strips in this book are reproduced by permission of United Feature Syndicate, Inc.

Visit our Web site at www.writersdigest.com for information on more resources for writers.

To receive a free weekly E-mail newsletter delivering tips and updates about writing and about Writer's Digest products, register directly at our Web site at http://newsletters.fwpublications.com.

06 05 04 03 02   5 4 3 2 1

Library of Congress Cataloging-in-Publication Data
Snoopy's guide to the writing life/ edited by Barnaby Conrad ; with a foreword by Monte Schulz.
    p.   cm
    ISBN 1-58297-194-3
    Schulz, Charles M. Peanuts. 2. Snoopy (Fictitious character). 3. Authorship. I. Conrad, Barnaby

    PN6728.P4 S32757 2002
    808'.02—dc21   2002028861

Edited by Donya Dickerson
Designed by Wendy Dunning
Interior layout by Cheryl VanDeMotter
Production coordinated by Sara Dumford

To Sparky, with love

Table of Contents

Foreword

Monte Schulz

My father loved reading, and he adored the literary arts. His office walls were lined with three thousand volumes on myriad topics, and the side table by his reading chair at home always had a further stack of books waiting to be read. He admired many a passage from those works he loved best—the famous scene of the tortoise crossing the road in John Steinbeck's *The Grapes of Wrath* or those great torrid paragraphs from Thomas Wolfe's wonderful novels of America. Oddly enough, although my father wrote and drew his comic strip for fifty years, he never considered himself a writer. Instead, he regarded "book writing" as a higher form of art than his beloved cartooning, which he always believed to be primarily a commercial venture. That did not prevent him, however, from adapting literature's many influences into his own unique art. He was intrigued by language, those lovely sentences and clever turns of phrases, that have always made the written word so beguiling to readers of all ages. He once told me that the poet's gift and artistic responsibility is to express the sorrow and beauty of life for those who cannot: a jilted lover who finds solace in a book of poetry or a traveler discovering the secret route to an undiscovered country in the ancient journals of those who have gone before. We read to hear these voices and learn from them.

When I was young, my father gave me some of his favorite adventure books to read, like *Driscoll's Book of Pirates* and *Red Rackham's Treasure*. He wanted me to become as entranced by the storyteller's art as he was. When we watched W.C. Fields in *The Bank Dick*, my father imitated his cigar-smoking, child-loathing hero: "Get away, kid, you're bothering me." He loved the snickering language of those movies. He persuaded me to read H.G. Wells and Jules Verne and Edgar Rice Burroughs. Being a veteran of the Second World War, my father loved Bill Mauldin's Willie and Joe, and he gave me Ernie Pyle's correspondences and the collected volumes of *Yank*. His own reading was astoundingly eclectic. He loved poetry and prose, fiction and non-fiction. When I was younger, he read the Bible and Bible commentaries and taught Sunday School at the Methodist church. He studied and discussed the finer points of theological issues with friends ("It seems to me the truest verse in the Bible is found in Hosea where the Lord says He requires mercy, and not sacrifice").

My father's life seemed in many ways to exemplify the love of artistic expression. His studio always had a record player so that on any work day he could listen to Brahms, Beethoven, and Tennessee Ernie Ford. He adored the art of both Andrew Wyeth and George Herriman's *Krazy Kat*. Perhaps because he always felt comic strips were a lesser art form, a commercial enterprise, he had a true affection for popular culture, even as he aspired to a great appreciation of the finer

...er... stormy knight.

It was a dark and stormy Christmas night,

meanwhile on a small farm in ...sas, a boy was growing up.

End of Part I

climbed into ...rriage, he ... goodbye.

"How can I take you anyplace when it's a dark and stormy night?" he said.

Call me Ishmael.

...ddenly, their dog, Rex, ...cided he'd better ...ke over!

...ent."

It was a dark and stormy night

...e also said, ...ave a nice day!"

By Supper Possessed

...ir eyes met... ...e minutes later ...y were married.

...a crowded ...e was lonely

arts. When I was a boy, he insisted I read Robert Louis Stevenson's *Kidnapped,* then sat with me on the living room sofa to watch the film version of it with Jackie Cooper whenever it aired on television. We read baseball stories together from *Boys' Life* magazine and talked about *Beau Geste* and the French Foreign Legion.

Later, as Snoopy's imagination carried him to distant places and times in his own pursuit of glory and adventure, I suppose I saw where many of my father's keenest desires lay. Years later, it seems to me that his heart was constantly divided between these two camps—the popular arts of mass culture and the rarefied aesthetic of literature, painting, and classical music. And certainly *Peanuts* was his own attempt to bridge that divide, to bring what he believed to be higher art into the world of the common reader. So Linus quoted Bible scripture while trying to organize theological debates on the pitcher's mound, Schroeder played Beethoven, and Snoopy read Tolstoy and chased the Red Baron across the skies of his own extravagant imagination. By doing so, *Peanuts* itself became more than popular art, speaking both to the daily reader and the dedicated artist, while appearing in both 2,600 daily newspapers around the globe and in its own exhibition in the Louvre.

Once I'd reached the age where literary art is appreciated as much as bravado storytelling, my father began recommending literary books for me to read. Years later he told me that one of his fondest wishes had been that one day I'd grow into an appreciation of literature so he and I could share and discuss the same books, some he would find to read, some I'd share with him. And finally we did. When I'd gone beyond reading science fiction and history, and discovered in college an interest in poetry and songwriting, I could tell I'd caught my father's attention. When I

told him how much I admired the lyricism in Paul Simon and Neil Young, he gave me *The Complete Poems of Carl Sandburg* and Edgar Lee Masters's *Spoon River Anthology*. He loved both of these volumes, and Sandburg eventually exerted the most pervasive influence in my own writing style. Of course, once my father had loaned these books to me, there was no hope of his ever seeing them again, but he didn't seem to mind. He gave me his own copies of Joan Didion's *Slouching Towards Bethlehem* and John Steinbeck's *East of Eden*. Once I began writing poetry in earnest, he brought me with him to the Santa Barbara Writer's Conference and enrolled me in the workshops there where I read a long epic poem I'd written on California. What made me proudest that year was not so much how enthusiastically my work was received but by how proud my father seemed to be. From then on, I had no greater fan of my writing than my own father, no one who supported me more than him. Likewise, as I grew older, I came to an even greater appreciation of his work, too.

This book ought to provide the reader with a good insight into many of the writers my father most admired. He was a big fan of Leo Tolstoy and believed *War and Peace* to be perhaps the greatest novel ever written. He also loved Thomas Hardy's books and much of Charles Dickens and Jane Austen, as well as the literature of the Bible. He was fortunate (or perhaps it was deliberate) to have a medium—*Peanuts*—in which he was able to quote from and make allusions to his favorite writers and artists, to draw parallels between their work and his own. And, again, these were not simple writers he found on bookshelves or whose works he'd read years and years before and remembered only by title and theme. In fact, he spoke constantly of his admiration for *Ethan Frome* and *War and Peace* and the Old Testament books of Job and Ecclesiastes, and

her... stormy knight.

It was dark and Chris...

anwh... ll farm in ...sas, ...owing up.

End of Part I

e climbed into carriage, he ...ed goodbye.

Call me Ishmael.

"How can I take you anyplace when it's a dark and stormy night?" he said.

uddenly, their dog, Rex, decided he'd better ...ke over!

erent," ...ll

It was a dark and stormy night

He also said, Have a nice day!"

By Supper Possessed

heir eyes met... ive minutes later ey were married.

s a crowded ...e was lonely.

he suggested these books to friends and acquaintances looking for something interesting and worthwhile to read. They were easy choices for my father because of how much he loved these authors. Every writer who's ever made the written word his or her passion in life has literary antecedents, mentors or models or heroes or templates for writing. We need our favorites both to inspire and motivate us, to offer something to aspire to, aim for, and emulate in our way. Clearly my father drew from not only the cartoonists of his childhood, but those literary figures whose achievements he considered far beyond his own and whose inspiration led him to create a work of art that eventually reached its own lofty heights.

Yet it's also important to point out that my father didn't just read and reread the authors of his youth. Indeed, he spent a great many afternoons after work frequenting the bookstores of his hometown. For an hour or so, he'd browse through all the newest titles in fiction and nonfiction, constantly on the lookout for something to catch his attention. Rarely would he leave a bookstore without buying two or three books, often more. Impatient as he was intrigued, he'd read half a dozen books at a time, dipping in each one to see what held his attention and entertained or provided him both with ideas and further inspiration for his daily strip. As an example of how eclectic his reading was, here are just a handful of the books on his office shelves: _Beau Geste; The Human Comedy; In Flanders Fields; Point of No Return; The Bobby Jones Story; Thurber and Company; The Reader's Bible; Rabbit, Run; Valentines; The French Foreign Legion; One Way to Spell Man; The Death of a President; Grant Moves South; The World of the Past; The War Lover; Agee on Film; Hans Brinker; The Interpreters Bible; They Also Ran; An Unfinished Woman; The Dragons of Eden; The Great Gatsby; Apostles of Discord; The Bogey Man;_

Beloved Infidel; Ibsen; The Bridge Player's Bedside Companion; The Big Knock-Over; Ernie Pyle's War; Back Home; Max Perkins; The Gathering Storm; Caesar and Christ; Beethoven: Biography of a Genius; Short Stories From The New Yorker; *You Shall Be As Gods; The Complete Sherlock Holmes; The Caine Mutiny; Anna Karenina; To the Lighthouse; The Yearling; Wonderland; The Man Who Played God; August 1914.*

This was where I was finally able to share his love of literature and ideas. We read many of the same books while also talking about those we didn't enjoy in common. He introduced me to the novels of Thomas Wolfe by having me read those great lyric passages like "Go, seeker, if you will, throughout the land and you will find us burning in the night . . . " from *You Can't Go Home Again* and the famous train sequence in *Of Time and the River*. Later, while reading novels of the Jazz Age as research for my second novel, I discovered John Dos Passos's *U.S.A.*, and within a week my father was reading it, too. We talked about this great American novel for six months. I think *U.S.A.* was the first book I'd ever suggested that my father read and enjoyed. After that, however, we found several authors we both admired and discussed: James Lee Burke's crime novels, Joseph Mitchell's *New Yorker* pieces, Carl Hiaasen's funny Florida novels, and the Border Trilogy of Cormac McCarthy, a writer we both decided was as gifted as any we'd ever read.

Certainly we didn't share all our favorite authors in common. He loved English writers, and I preferred American. He enjoyed leisurely paced literary novels, while I'd read both literary and popular fiction. I persuaded him to try Stephen King's *Misery*, and though he enjoyed it, he didn't love it as much as I did, which I found somewhat interesting. Here was a fan of comic strips,

adventure stories, and movie serials from his youth who didn't thrill as I did to *Star Wars* and *Aliens*, or the novels of John Grisham and Michael Crichton. Yet I suppose both our tastes were schizophrenic in that way, since I loved Stephen King and James Joyce, Robert McCammon and William Faulkner, while he preferred Anita Brookner, A.S. Byatt, and Elmore Leonard. Indeed, we both read for art and entertainment. Maybe some of that had to do with which works provided the greatest influence on our writing. My father adored Laurel and Hardy, but there's more Shakespeare and Leo Tolstoy in his comic strip, more Thomas Hardy than Harold Lloyd. We glean what we can from the authors whose achievements seem most remarkable to us, but we also read for fun and go to the movies to escape the real world and lose ourselves in another place and time. My father loved the cinema even as he believed there can be no such thing as great art by committee. Therefore, he admired Woody Allen as a writer and actor and director, while enjoying Steven Spielberg's *Close Encounters of the Third Kind* for the entertainment it truly was. We often debated the merits of movies and television shows we liked, each to his own preference, never quite gaining headway in each other's favorites. So I still liked *Raiders of the Lost Ark* much better than *Upstairs, Downstairs*, yet we were both brought to tears by Horton Foote's wonderful *Trip to Bountiful*. No father and son shared a deeper appreciation of this mutual adoration of art and the written word. It bound us together for the last years of my father's life, made us pals once again as we'd been in those long-ago days of throwing the baseball after dinner in a summer twilight.

My father told me once that the truest benefit of fame was gaining the opportunity to meet many of the people he admired most in the world. As I said earlier, he never thought of himself as a true writer. He didn't consider the comic strip as high an art form as the novel or stage plays. He always looked up to writers of literary fiction as sojourners in a greater calling. I think he enjoyed being in the community of artists and writers, even as he pursued his own art in the most solitary fashion, creating his own ideas, drawing the strip every day, doing his own lettering. He was keenly aware of both his contemporaries and his artistic antecedents. He loved talking about writing and meeting writers. In 1967 Barnaby Conrad interviewed him for *The New York Times Magazine,* and five years later, my father traveled to Southern California to take part in Barnaby's Santa Barbara Writer's Conference with Ray Bradbury, Budd Schulberg, James Michener, Alex Haley, and a community of students. Nearly every June for twenty-five years afterward he visited the conference where he was asked to speak on what it meant to be a writer. It humbled him to be invited to share his views on the literary life, given that he never truly considered himself one of that crowd. It was also fascinating to see how he handled his own fame in a forum with writers of renown. While he treated distinguished authors like Anne Lamott with great deference and humility, he seemed often only vaguely aware of the awe with which they regarded him. Almost as if he didn't accept the idea that fame in his own artistic endeavors gained him notoriety in a companion forum, he spoke fondly of the achievements of writers he admired and only grudgingly acknowledged how thrilled they were to have the opportunity of meeting him. Of course, he was perfectly aware of his own astounding success. Indeed, he once told a story of dining with my older sister at a restaurant in Mexico and noticing behind him at another table screen legends Elizabeth Taylor and Richard Burton. He remarked to my sister how great it would be to meet them, to just go over and introduce himself and tell them how much he admired their work, but, of course, they probably wouldn't know who he was (a lowly cartoonist?), and he'd feel as though he'd intruded on their evening. Just then, from behind him, he heard a voice say, "Mr. Schulz?" Turning around, my father said he saw both Richard Burton and Elizabeth Taylor standing there. Richard Burton said, "We don't want to disturb you, but we're both big fans of yours and wanted to meet you."

Although my father was certainly aware of his own fame, he always said somehow he felt like a fraud at the Santa Barbara Writer's Conference. He'd give his talk and enjoy his week there in the company of fellow writers, but in between conferences, he'd resolve not to return, believing that he didn't really have that much to offer other writers and that, in any event, certainly people were tired of hearing him speak. Of course he was wrong. In the couple years or so he was absent from the conference, I was deluged with requests to persuade him to return, and it was difficult to imagine anyone missed more than him. The auditorium was always full for his talk, and his audience was enthusiastic; they loved hearing what he had to say about the artist's life and how they might benefit by that long journey he made from the obscurity of a shy barber's son who liked drawing funny pictures to becoming the most famous and successful cartoonist of the twentieth century. What was most evident in hearing him speak was how much he enjoyed what he created, and his enthusiasm was shared with the many aspiring writers he met during his annual week at the conference. I used to remind him that doing this was fun, that he always relaxed and thrived in a community of artists and authors. So I think attending the conference was good for him, too. Not only did it give him a brief and comfortable vacation away from his day-to-day routine, but it also offered him the opportunity to talk about books and writing, to rediscover that simple passion for the written word, the art of literature—no small reward.

Snoopy perched in front of a typewriter on his famous doghouse is one of the enduring images of *Peanuts*. His flights of literary imagination take hold of every writer and remind us (as if we needed reminding) that once we admit to ourselves we require and adore the written word and the writer's life, we are bound to chase that ever elusive perfect sentence, paragraph, story, novel, poem. Rejections, blocks, false starts, and dead ends only distract us; they cannot lead us away from this holy destiny we know is ours. Without a doubt, my father used Snoopy the author to express his own love and frustration with the creative process, to illuminate the writer's life by poking fun at the often incomprehensible divide between author and publisher while showing the amazing resilience of the everyday writer struggling for acceptance and acknowledgment. Some know fame and others anonymity, but my father believed there were no shortcuts to be had in the life of the dedicated artist. There is only faith and persistence. In the last days of his life, my father knew that his own commitment to the art of the written word had been honest and complete, and when he passed from this world, he left as a writer. We should all be so fortunate.

Monte Schulz
Nevada City, California

Introduction

Barnaby Conrad

I once asked Charles Schulz what was his favorite of all the thousands of *Peanuts* cartoons he had drawn over fifty years.

"I can't pick a favorite," he said. "But the one that has drawn the most mail was a Sunday one, and Snoopy wasn't even in it."

The three kids are standing on a little hill looking up at the sky. Lucy says, "Aren't the clouds beautiful? They look like big balls of cotton . . ."

In the next panel she says, "I could just lie here all day, and watch them drift by . . ."

In the following panel she adds, "If you use your imagination, you can see lots of things in the cloud formations . . . What do you think you see, Linus?"

And he says, "Well, those clouds up there look to me like the map of the British Honduras on the Caribbean . . . that cloud up there looks a little like the profile of Thomas Eakins, the famous painter and sculptor . . . and that group of clouds over there gives me the impression of the stoning of Stephen . . . I can see the Apostle Paul standing there to one side . . ."

And Lucy says, "Uh, huh . . . that's very good . . . What do *you* see in the clouds, Charlie Brown?"

And the hapless Charlie says, "Well, I was going to say I saw a ducky and a horsie, but I changed my mind!"

Schulz told me the only idea he ever used that came directly from his own children was once when his young daughter, Amy, was "jabbering away at the dinner table and I said, 'Can't you

please be quiet?' And she was silent for a moment and then picked up a slice of bread and began to butter it, saying, 'Am I buttering too loud for you?' I gave the line to Linus after Lucy yells at him."

But I believe Schulz got many ideas from coming to our annual Santa Barbara Writer's Conference for his cherished series of Snoopy at the typewriter from our students, all struggling like the Beagle, to get published. "Sparky" attended all but a few of the almost three decades of conferences, and he would stay all week, not just the day he spoke, and he would attend every lecture and visit almost every workshop in the many different genres.

On the day he lectured, usually to five hundred people, he would always draw a huge cartoon on an illustration board (usually of Snoopy at the typewriter) "just to prove to you that I am who I say I am."

He would then give the big drawing—plus dozens of original strips—for auction for scholarships to our conference.

I believe that Snoopy was the favorite of all his characters, perhaps because he was based on the beloved pet he had in his childhood in Minnesota.

"Snoopy's not a real dog, of course—he's an image of what people would like a dog to be. But he has his origins in Spike, my dog that I had when I was a kid. White with black spots. He was the wildest and smartest dog I've ever encountered. Smart? Why, he had a vocabulary of at least fifty words. I mean it. I'd tell him to go down to the basement and bring up a potato, and he'd do it. I used to chip tennis balls at him, and he'd catch and retrieve 'em. He really understood language, which Snoopy does. Notice that Snoopy doesn't speak ever, but he understands everything the kids say. Snoopy often ignores the fact that he's a dog. I did a strip once where Charlie Brown, reading from the newspaper, says, 'It says here they're having a dog show. Have you ever thought of entering a dog show?' and Snoopy thinks, 'How could I? I don't even *own* a dog!'"

We take Snoopy for granted, at or not at, his typewriter. But where did he come from?

In a Sunday panel in 1972, Linus asks Charlie Brown, "How did you happen to get Snoopy, Charlie Brown?" Charlie replies, "Well, I'm not quite sure because I was kind of young. I think it started because of something that happened at a playground . . . I was playing in a sandbox with a couple of other kids . . . I can't even remember who they were . . . Anyway, all of a sudden, one of them poured a whole bucket of sand over my head . . . I started crying, I guess, and my mother came running up, and took me home—it's kind of embarrassing now to talk about it.

"Anyway, the next day we drove out to the Daisy Hill Puppy Farm, and my mother and dad bought me a dog."

And Snoopy, lying on his doghouse on his back, eyes closed, mutters—what else?—"Good Grief!"

So that's where Snoopy came from. But where did author Snoopy, the would-be canine Tolstoy, come from?

Where did the far-fetched idea of a dog sitting on his doghouse typing stories come from? For that matter, where did all his ideas come from? Jean, Schulz's second wife of twenty-five years, wrote:

"The essence of his genius is: We can't know it, quantify it, explain it; we can, simply, enjoy it. If those of us who are part of his circle puzzle over the questions and struggle for answers, no one struggled more than Sparky himself.

"He understood intuitively things he couldn't explain. Things he couldn't even put into words. He could go only so far as to answer the perennial question, 'Where do your ideas come from?'

"The ideas Sparky used are out there in the world. We all know them, and that is why we relate to them. It is the particular twist Sparky put to the ideas that described his genius, and that draws us, enchanted, into his frame.

"I believe there are people of genius around us, but few are fortunate enough to have their genius match the moment. A thousand years ago, Sparky would have been a storyteller, the person in the tribe or the clan who collected the tribal lore and repeated it for each generation. He understood instinctively the value of the story which illustrates a human truth and which allows his listeners to take from it what they need at the time. The best stories can be told over and over again—forever new—because the listener changes."

I first met the cartoonist in 1967 when I went up to his house near Sebastopol, an hour north of San Francisco, to interview him for *The New York Times Magazine*.

And what a house and layout it was: over the twenty-eight acres—horses, golf holes, swimming pool, baseball diamond, tennis courts—a studio separate from the house, and not so far away in Santa Rosa, his own hockey rink.

I started out asking the friendly Mr. Schulz ("call me Sparky, please") if he thought of himself as a frustrated writer and/or painter.

16

"No," he said. "I've just always wanted to be a cartoonist, and I'm happy to be just that. Cartooning is a *fairly* sort of a proposition. You have to be fairly intelligent—if you were really intelligent you'd be doing something else; you have to draw fairly well—if you drew really well you'd be a painter; you have to write fairly well—if you wrote really well you'd be writing books. It's great for a fairly person like me."

For a fairly sort of person, Schulz bid fair to be the most recognized and successful and beloved cartoonist of all time. It was said at the time of this death (February 12, 2000) that with his cartoon strip and the products and greeting cards and films, "The *Peanuts* Industry" brought in some 30 million dollars annually. (As far back as 1962 and 1963, the book *Happiness Is a Warm Puppy* was on *The New York Times's* best-seller list for forty-five weeks.)

Yet "Sparky" Schulz remained modest, unassuming, and simple with it all. I asked him if he, like many cartoonists today, had an assistant to help him draw, do the lettering, or ink in the penciled drawings.

"Good grief, no," he replied. "The two things I like to do best in this life are drawing and golfing, and if I hired someone to do my strip for me it would be like my hiring someone to hit my golf balls for me."

He liked to talk about the strip and cartooning in general which, despite his "fairly" dissertation, he considered a high form of art.

"I like the violent action ones, kids getting bowled over and such things that cartoons were born to do. Too many of these new strips are not cartoons—they're imitations of films, and the movies can do it so much better, beat them at their own game. But I like the quiet ones, too. I like it when Linus says, simply, 'Sucking your thumb without a blanket is like eating a cone without ice cream.' I like non sequiturs, like the time Lucy is giving a dissertation on butterflies and points out a species of Brazilian butterfly on the ground to Linus. 'That's a potato chip,' he says. Undaunted, Lucy says, 'How do you suppose that potato chip got here from Brazil?' I like it when Charlie Brown gets all excited about a big spelling bee and then goes out on the first word because they say, 'Spell "maze,"' and, being the good baseball fan he is, he spells it 'Mays.' I like to keep it all simple. For instance, it seems to me that Snoopy's been getting pretty fantastical lately. I think I'll simplify him, let him just be a dog for a while."

The phone rang, and he talked for a few minutes. When he hung up he said, "That was something about having a helicopter be attacked by the Red Baron. Over Chicago. They've got a real German World War I plane. Publicity stunt of some kind." He shook his head incredulously, and a little sheepishly, at the world he had created. "Where's it all going to end?"

Charles Monroe Schulz, as every good *Peanuts* aficionado knows, was born in Minneapolis, Minnesota, in 1922. When he was two days old, he was nicknamed "Sparky" by his family for Barney Google's horse Sparkplug, and called that by his family and friends. From almost the beginning he wanted to become a cartoonist, thinking it among the noblest of the artistic professions.

"It's a great art," he would say. "I'm convinced it's much harder and more important than illustration. Look at that"—he pointed to a framed original cartoon page of *Krazy Kat* by George Herriman—"that's art. It was done around 1912, and its humor is every bit as fresh today as then."

18

Sparky's early life was very Charlie Brownish. "People read a lot into the strip, and I guess what people see in it, that's what's in it. But actually the strip is just about all the dumb things I did when I was little."

In fine Charlie Brown fashion, he was the goat on the baseball field, once losing a game forty to nothing, and even his drawings were turned down by the high-school yearbook. In the army he was similarly unsuccessful. After being trained as a machine gunner, he discovered he had forgotten to load his weapon the one and only time he was confronted by members of the enemy forces while fighting in World War II.

"It was the last week of the war, and we were going along a road in southern Germany in a halftrack and somebody said, 'Hey—look over there, there's somebody in that hole over there in the field, shoot him.' So I swung the gun around—.50-caliber—pressed the butterfly trigger, and nothing happened. Before I could load he came out with his hands up, and I was sure glad I hadn't been able to shoot him."

After the war he got a job lettering a comic magazine, then taught in a Minneapolis art school of the "Draw-me-and-win-a-scholarship" mail-order variety. A fellow instructor was named Charlie Brown and later unwittingly lent his name to posterity. Another had a pretty blue-eyed sister named Joyce Halverson, and Schulz married her. In 1948 he sold his first cartoon to *The Saturday Evening Post*. Then he did a weekly cartoon for the *St. Paul Pioneer Press* called *Li'l Folks*. Within a year it was dropped. After many rejections from other syndicates, it was picked up by United Features in Manhattan. Over Schulz's protests it was renamed *Peanuts*.

"What an ugly word it is," he said disgustedly. "Say it: Peanuts! I can't stand to even write it. And it's a terrible title. Now 'Peppermint Patty' is a good title for a strip. I introduced a character named that into the strip to keep someone else from using it. Funny, people don't tell you how to draw or write, but *everybody* is an expert on titles."

The first month Schultz made ninety dollars with his newly titled strip. A few months later it was up to one thousand dollars a month. Twenty years later it was one thousand dollars a day.

"Funny," Sparky said to me, "I never set out to do a cartoon about kids. I just wanted to be a good cartoonist, like, say, Herriman or my boyhood idol, Roy Crane, who draws *Buz Sawyer*— a fine cartoonist. I always dreamed of some day coming up with some permanent idea or phrase that would pass into the language, like Snuffy Smith's 'bodacious' or some of Al Capp's gimmicks. I guess maybe 'Good grief' has made it. And perhaps the Great Pumpkin. And the *Happiness Is* . . . title.

"There were a lot of good cartoonists around. I read all of 'em. Capp, Caniff, 'Miss Peach.' It pleases me that my children seem to like *Peanuts* as well as any of the others. They know all the books by heart and have favorite strips on their walls and play the records. It's all very gratifying."

Many psychiatrists who charge a good deal more than Lucy Van Pelt's five-cent consultation fee have tried to analyze the special appeal of *Peanuts*. My pedestrian conclusion is that Schulz felt the loss of his dog Spike as deeply as he did a quarter of a century ago, just as he felt the loss of his childhood. Happily for the readers, he was able to translate this long memory and deep feeling into words and pictures. It seems to be universal, either because we had a childhood like that, or wish we had. There's a little Charlie Brown in all of us males and, Lord knows, we've all known, and maybe even married, a Lucy Van Pelt, a girl who shouts, "I don't want any downs—I just want ups and ups and ups!" Certainly there's been someone in each one of our lives ready and eager to pull away the metaphorical football just as we're about to kick it.

Schulz said in 1966, "Little girls of that age are smarter than little boys, and Lucy knows it better than most little girls. But she's not as smart as she thinks she is. Beneath the surface there's something tender. But perhaps if you scratched deeper, you'd find she's even worse than she seems."

So very often the strip touches chords that remind us of things and homely events we thought we had forgotten. As the catalog for a Whitney exhibition of Andrew Wyeth (Schulz's favorite painter, along with Picasso) stated, "But art arises in the human spirit beyond the reach of words from the levels of deepest memories. We are creatures who need the near and the familiar as well as the exotic."

Emerson wrote in 1838, "A man must have aunts and cousins, must buy carrots and turnips, must have barn and woodshed, must go to market and to the blacksmith's shop, must saunter and sleep and be inferior and silly."

Sparky once said, "All the loves in the strip are unrequited, all the baseball games are lost, all the test scores D-minuses, the Great Pumpkin never comes, and the football is always pulled away."

Most readers don't think about the fact that grown-ups never appear in the strip—the strictly kids' world. But once, way back in 1954, Schulz did four Sunday golf panels on the kids with grown-ups in the background of a tournament. He quickly realized his mistake—a kind of shattering of the illusion of a very special world—and never repeated it.

Another factor in the strip's popularity with all ages is his sublime handling of how far the fantasy should go. For example, Snoopy's doghouse is always shown in profile; we never see a three-quarters view or actually go inside it. We just accept the fact when it is said that Snoopy has a Wyeth and a Van Gogh and a pool table in there, but if we actually saw inside and discovered an unbelievable doghouse, we would cease to believe in Snoopy as a dog and his relationship with the children. Another all-important factor in Schulz's astonishingly good batting average is his unfailing sense of what is subtly funny.

"I get letters all the time," he told me, "from optometrists saying, 'How come you're always talking about ophthalmologists'—Linus wore glasses, you know—'Why not give *us* a break?' It's hard to tell them that 'ophthalmology' is somehow funny and the word 'optometry' just isn't. Like Beethoven. My favorite composer is Brahms—I could listen to him all day—but Brahms isn't a funny word. Beethoven is, so I gave him to Schroeder. I like names: Linus is a good name. I borrowed that from a friend, Linus Maurer. Funny, the other night I was trying to think of a good last name for Pigpen—he hasn't got one—and I fell asleep and I dreamed of a new character named José Peterson. That's a good name, isn't it? But I only put him in the strip for a week—he was a baseball player—but he just didn't belong, so out he went, along with some others I've gotten rid of. My strip is not like the kind that depends on variety or new characters. I've got pretty much the same characters and basic idea that I had so many years ago. I want to keep the strip simple. I like it, for example, when Charlie Brown watches the first leaf of fall float down and then walks over and just says, 'Did you have a good summer?' That's the kind of strip that gives me pleasure to do.

"I usually get between four and five hundred letters a week, and for years I've managed to answer all of them personally, but I don't know." He leafed through some of the letters. "Most of them are so nice, and their requests are so polite and worthwhile—a drawing for a crippled kid, a poster for a special high-school dance. 'Just do a quick sketch of Snoopy,' they ask. 'It'll only take five minutes.' And they're right—it *would* only take five minutes. But they think their letter is the only one on my desk. The five minutes have to be multiplied by hundreds." He looked mournfully at the heap of mail. "Thousands. They forget that I not only have to do some drawing. I occasionally have to do some thinking."

He looked out of his studio window and studied a clump of trees beyond an artificial pond. "It's hard to convince people when you're just staring out of the window that you're doing your hardest work of the day. In fact, many times when I'm just sitting here thinking and therefore working like heck, I hear the door open and I quickly grab the pen and a piece of paper and start drawing something so that people won't think I'm just goofing off and anxious to have a little chat. But I like visitors when I'm drawing. It gets lonely up here all day, not like an office or a dentist or somebody who has company around him all the time." Schulz was termed a recluse but he said, "Oh, we go to San Francisco about once a month, see friends, go to a play. But we aren't night-clubbers or cocktail types. Neither of us drink, never have, just isn't part of our life, and our friends just have to accept us like that."

He picked up some more letters. "Lots of people write in ideas. Some are good, but I don't seem to be able to use other people's suggestions. Yesterday I had a pretty good one—'Why not have Snoopy pretend he's a Grand Prix racing driver?' Now that's not a bad idea, and I guess it

23

would work. But I didn't think of it; I'd just be imitating myself. Wasn't it Somerset Maugham who said, 'Imitate others if you must, but when you start imitating yourself, you're through.'"

Schulz began his day at 9:30 by walking the quarter mile from his sprawling one-level house across the lawns of his golf holes, past the big swimming pool to his studio. With a secretary in the outer office and a plush living room before one arrived at the place where he actually drew, it could very well have been the office of a successful real-estate broker or a pre-need cemetery-lot salesman.

Clinically neat and organized, Schulz would sit at the drawing board and began by playing around on a scratch pad with a pencil, doodling situations and ideas. He tried to conceive of the week's work as a whole; six separate day's drawings that would somehow make a unity. When he had the ideas fairly well set in his mind he would take a twenty-eight-inch illustration board, which had the margins of the four panels printed on it already, and ink in the dialogue. When he had all six day's strips "dialogued in," he began to draw the figures and the action, preferring to draw directly with the pen with a minimum of penciled guidelines.

One day's strip took him about an hour to draw. The Sunday page took the whole day.

"All you're trying to do is fill in those squares," he said in 1999. "Do something good for Monday and then do something good for Tuesday and then you do something for Wednesday. Where does it all come from?"

Even though it has been some two years since his death, many people still are unaware of it since the strip appears in all the same papers—reruns of course, but who cares? Snoopy, Charlie,

24

Linus, Lucy, and the gang will never grow old—why should we? Snoopy will be at his typewriter long after people even remember what a typewriter was.

Yes, they say Charles Schulz died in the year 2000, the day before his very last strip ran. But I like to think the way novelist John O'Hara did when he heard about his friend George Gershwin's going: "George Gershwin died yesterday. I don't have to believe it if I don't want to."

Monte Schulz and I wish to thank the many outstanding writers who in this book have shared their expertise and reactions to Snoopy's literary musings and attempts to write The Great American Novel. Only a couple of authors declined, for various reasons, our invitation to contribute an essay. The best was from the distinguished writer John Updike. In a kindly note he wrote: "As Snoopy would tell you, a writer hates to return a check, but I have never been good at giving advice to other writers. If I knew something that would make a crucial difference, I would keep it to myself, since the field is so overcrowded."

Sorry, Snoopy!

Barnaby Conrad
Carpinteria, California

It

It was

It was a
dark

It was a
dark and
stormy night.

GOOD WRITING IS
HARD WORK!

7-13

Danielle Steel

I'm glad that Snoopy so early in his career has learned that very important truth—good writing (and even bad writing)—is hard work. Very hard work.

This business is fraught with uncertainty. Anyone who tells you how to write best-sellers is a sham and a liar. I can tell you how I write books. I write them with fear, excitement, discipline, and a lot of hard work. It takes me a year to write the outline and about a month to write the first draft. For me that's the shortest part of the process. But that's a matter of twenty-two-hour days, of not leaving my house or my office, of not speaking to my friends, or speaking to anyone other than my children. All I do is write. And the cleaning up process, i.e., the editing, after that is roughly another eighteen months. So the whole process takes me about two and a half years.

Where do the ideas come from? I don't really know. I've always had a deeply religious feeling about my writing. I feel very unimportant in the scheme of it all. I pray a lot before I start a book and as I work through it. And the less important I feel, the better the book goes.

The story comes from somewhere and seems to flow through me until it's finished. And I myself am in awe of the finished product as it sits there, five hundred pages high on my desk. But I don't feel personally responsible for it. I never feel entirely sure I did it. I just seem to be part of the process—the window the light shines through.

The only part of the process I am absolutely sure of is the discipline involved. For me writing is a job, a career. It has been for years. It is not an artistic pastime. I don't wait for inspiration to come at three in the morning. I sit down with my notebook and my pen at nine in the morning and force myself to sit there, working on an idea for hours.

I work and I think and I push and I scribble until something comes. When I actually get something to work on, I sit at my typewriter and type until I ache so badly I can't get up. After twelve or fourteen hours, you feel as if your whole body is going to break in half. Everything hurts—your arms, your eyes, your shoulders, your neck, your hands. I've had cramps so badly when I sat typing that I couldn't move my hands for a couple hours, but I usually keep sitting there and push through it for another five or six hours.

And after a while my whole body goes numb, and all I'm aware of is the story I'm writing. I hear it in my head. I see it in front of me like a film, and I type what I see and hear.

I have often typed so long that I saw double. I have had to close my eyes to keep typing because my vision was so blurred. I have fallen asleep face first in my typewriter and woken up the next morning with the keyboard marks on my face.

But the aches and the agonies no longer matter. It feels wonderful. The feeling of accomplishment, of victory, of survival is overwhelming. It's a little bit like a marathon or climbing a mountain.

Snoopy might think about choosing another, easier calling, but I doubt if he (or I) ever will.

Danielle Steel *is considered one of the best-selling novelists of all time; she has sold five hundred million books in the United States alone.*

30

It was a dark and stormy night. Suddenly, a shot rang out!

11-19 © 1981 United Feature Syndicate, Inc.

ISN'T THERE ENOUGH VIOLENCE IN THE WORLD TODAY?

CAN'T YOU WRITE ABOUT SOMETHING NICE?

It was a dark and stormy night. Suddenly, a kiss rang out!

Some nights were dark. Some nights were stormy.

7-13 © 1991 United Feature Syndicate, Inc.

Some shots rang out. Some maids screamed.

Some more editors sent rejection slips.

32

33

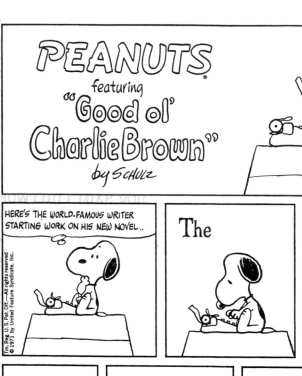

34

Panel 1: YOU SHOULD WRITE A "PAGE TURNER"

Panel 2: WRITE A BOOK THAT WILL "SWEEP BOOKSELLERS OFF THEIR FEET"

10-11

www.unitedmedia.com

Panel 3: YOU SHOULD WRITE A BOOK THAT IS "POWERFUL, YET HEARTWARMING!"

© 1996 United Feature Syndicate, Inc.

Panel 4: I'M HAVING TROUBLE WITH THE FIRST SENTENCE..

Clive Cussler

Snoopy, try this when you sit down to the typewriter: Just say to yourself, "What if?"

It all begins with "What if?"

What if they let pigs out in a mosque? What if they decide to change the name of Mexico to Schwartz? What if they start referring to whites as European Americans?

Then comes, Why would they do that? I have to figure out why. So if I have my beginning I can begin the story. I may not have a middle, but I must have an ending to work toward. I'm heavier on plot than characters. I cast characters like I was casting a movie. The villain has to really be nasty so the reader cheers when the hero does him in. The good guys have to be like friendly neighbors next door. They must be people you'd like to have a beer with, somebody a woman would feel comfortable with.

Then comes the scenes where you really put the characters through their paces. If mine were real, they'd hate me by the end of the book. I put them through so much hell it's a wonder any of

stormy knight.

It was a dark and stormy Christ

anwhile

sas, a

End of Part I

climbed into carriage, he d goodbye.

"How can I take you anyplace when it's a dark and stormy night?" he said.

Call me Ishmael.

ddenly, their dog Rex ecided he'd better ke over!

rent,"

It was a dark and stormy night

He also said, ave a nice day!"

By Supper

eir eyes met... Possessed

e minutes later y were married.

s a crowded

them survive to start the adventure all over again in the next book.

My biggest piece of advice is don't use desperately boring description to elaborate on something technical or dole out heavy explanation for nothing detail. The reader will ignore it and be bored. Describe it in dialogue. The vision in the mind of the reader flies so much faster, and the reader actually understands and enjoys hearing what the characters say about it.

My biggest piece of advice is don't use desperately boring description to elaborate on something technical or dole out heavy explanation for nothing detail. The reader will ignore it and be bored.

Just a few of **Clive Cussler's** best-sellers are Raise the Titanic!, Sahara, Inca Gold, Flood Tide, Cyclops, Treasure, Deep Six, *and* Iceberg.

38

PEANUTS The curtain of night enveloped the fleeing lovers. *7-31*

Though fiery trials had threatened, oceans of longing had kept them together.

Now, a new icicle of terror stabbed at the embroidery of their existence.

JOE METAPHOR!

PEANUTS And they lived happily ever after.

The End

FOR THE FIRST TIME IN MY LIFE, I KNOW HOW LEO MUST HAVE FELT... *9-8*

LEO TOLSTOY, THAT IS!

Sidney Sheldon

I met Charles Schulz one evening when we were both nominated for an Emmy (he won, I did not). That night, I told him how much I enjoyed the above cartoon. Two days later, I received the original drawing in the mail, signed to me with a warm inscription. I framed it, and it proudly hangs on the wall of my trophy room.

Snoopy is going through every writer's nightmare. *Is the idea worth writing about? Will the readers hate it? Am I wasting my time?* And there are no answers—until the book is published, and then it's too late.

The rules for writing a best-seller are simple:

- Take an idea you really, really like.
- Develop it until it is brilliant.
- Rewrite it for a year or two, until every word shines.

Then bite your nails, hold your breath, and pray like mad.

 Sidney Sheldon *has written dozens of screenplays and television scripts. He is also the author of the best-selling novels* The Other Side of Midnight, The Naked Face, *and* A Stranger in the Mirror.

40

PEANUTS

As he touched her hand, she sighed...

STOP RAINING ON MY NOVEL!

The light mist turned to rain.

The rain turned to snow.

The story turned to boring.

41

PEANUTS® featuring **"Good ol' CharlieBrown"** by SCHULZ

It was a dark and stormy night.

Suddenly, a shot rang out. A door slammed. The maid screamed.

Suddenly, a pirate ship appeared on the horizon!

While millions of people were starving, the king lived in luxury.

Meanwhile, on a small farm in Kansas, a boy was growing up.

Part II

IN PART TWO, I TIE ALL OF THIS TOGETHER...

42

Cherie Carter-Scott

Everyone, including Snoopy, seems to be writing a self-help book. Here are ten rules even Snoopy should follow in order to do it well.

1 **You must develop a concept.** Search your heart and soul for what *you* have to contribute. Remember, your book must help someone with something.

2 **Know your subject matter like a pro.** Whether it's through study, life experience, or interviewing those who know the subject better than you do, you must become thoroughly versed in what you will write.

The following text appears faintly in the background on the left side of the page:

her... stormy knight.

It was a dark
and stormy
Christmas...

...anwhi... ...farm in
...nsas, a... ...ing up.

End of Part 1

...e climbed into
...carriage, he
...ed goodbye.

"How can I take you
anyplace when it's a
dark and stormy night?"
he said.

Call me
Ishmael.

...uddenly, their dog, Rex,
...ecided he'd better
...ke over!

...erent,"
...ll

It was a dark
and stormy night

He also said,
Have a nice day!"

By Supper
Possessed

...heir eyes met...
...ive minutes later
...ey were married.

...s a crowded

3 **Determine what qualifies you.** More than a desire to write, you need to establish your credibility. Know for yourself what makes you an "authority" capable of commenting on this topic.

Search your heart and soul for what you have to contribute. Remember, your book must help someone with something.

4 **Find your "voice" (even if it's a bark, Snoopy!).** All of us have subpersonalities that want to be heard. The "right" voice has consistency and integrity, and stays connected to your reader.

5 **Your personal experiences may inspire the reader.** People who read self-help books are interested in the author's personal story. Building a bridge between your readers and you is a tool that can truly empower them.

6 **Decide what must be included.** What to keep and what to cut are important decisions. It is ultimately up to you to determine what is essential in order to communicate your message.

7 **Having true stories helps to illustrate points.** People learn through example. When you show, rather than tell, it opens a door for your reader to take important steps.

8 **Integrity means that you sincerely walk your talk.** The most powerful material comes from living what you espouse. This is the most difficult task of being a self-help author . . . being the living proof that what you say does work.

9 **Testimonials help establish credibility.** When people publicly endorse your book it demonstrates popularity and support of your work. Recognizable names do help.

10 **Writing the book is 20 percent of the job; marketing is the other 80 percent.** In order for people to know your book exists, you must get the word out. A brilliant book may be overlooked if the public doesn't know about it . . . you have to help yourself to ultimately help others.

 Cherie Carter-Scott's *best-seller* If Life is a Game, These are the Rules, *was given attention on the* Oprah Winfrey Show. *Since its publication, she has also written three more successful "life-enhancing" books.*

It was a dark and stormy night

Suddenly a shot rang out. A door slammed. The maid screamed. Suddenly a pirate ship appeared on the horizon. While millions of people were starving, the king lived in luxury.

Meanwhile, on a small farm in Kansas, a boy was growing up. End of Part I

Part II
A light snow was falling, and the little girl with the tattered shawl had not sold a violet all day.

At that very moment, a young intern at City Hospital was making an important discovery.

I MAY HAVE WRITTEN MYSELF INTO A CORNER...

Gone With the Wind III
The story of Rhett and Scarlett.

It was a dark and stormy marriage.

© 1988 United Feature Syndicate, Inc.

Gone With the Wind III
Rhett had to admit he missed Scarlett.

"I know what I'll do," he said. "I'll buy her a beagle!"

© 1988 United Feature Syndicate, Inc.

Dear Editor,
  I am sending you my latest novel.

Don't

Our magazine assumes no responsibility for unso-licited material.

Dear Cor
  Thank y
submittin
manuscrip
  regret tha
  does not s
  our prese
  needs.

First printing will be one copy.

Enclosed please find the manuscript of my new novel

Dear

Dear Editor,
  Why do you keep se
  my stories back

Dear Author,
  Congratulations! We have decided to publish your novel.

No such material wi
returned unless sub
with a self-addres
envelope and sufficient

n second thought...

You're supposed to print them, and make me rich and famous.

If
pr

Dear Contributor,

What is
with you

Actually, we don't regret it at all.

The Gift

PEANUTS featuring "Good ol' CharlieBrown" by Schulz

It was the holiday season.

She and her husband had decided to attend a performance of King Lear.

It was their first night out together in months.

During the second act one of the performers became ill.

The manager of the theater walked onto the stage, and asked, "Is there a doctor in the house?"

Her husband stood up, and shouted, "I have an honorary degree from Anderson College!"

It was at that moment when she decided not to get him anything for Christmas.

12-22

Schulz

48

those years in Paris were to be among the finest of her life.

Looking back, she once remarked, "Those years in Paris were among the finest of my life." That was what she said when she looked back upon those years in Paris

where she spent some of the finest years of her life.

I THINK THIS IS GOING TO NEED A LITTLE EDITING...

Thomas McGuane

Snoopy, it's never easy.

When the words don't come, try talking to yourself using any kind of mnemonic device to get yourself going, scribbling phrases, automatic writing, anything, but get something down. Then you go back and take a hard look with a more critical eye.

Robert Stone said that when you look at something you've written and you think it's wrong, well, it *is* wrong. That's the rule, and at that point you know as much about revision as anyone knows about revision.

I'm always amazed at young writers, or arriving writers of any age, at how difficult it is to explain to them that they have so many stories right in their hands, locked in their lives, in their relationships, maybe in their awful jobs—it's not on the Siberian frontier. There's no such thing as a whole experience for a writer; you don't have to go the rodeo circuit or fight bulls or do any of those things. You just have to write well and truly understand what your subject is. And the good thing is that the reader recognizes it the instant you do.

That's what is so fabulous about this thing called writing.

Thomas McGuane *is famous for his short stories and novels, including* To Skin a Cat, Ninety-two in the Shade, *and* The Cadence of Grass. *He has also written screenplays, including* Rancho Deluxe *and* The Missouri Breaks.

50

Leslie Dixon

We've suffered enough, Snoopy!

If you write compulsively, you wait, quivering, for one thing: the moment you are finally paid for something you've written. Then you're anointed—a "real" writer. Before that validation, you feel like you're looking across a forbidding medieval moat, and everyone but you is inside the castle, partying.

The check clears; the drawbridge comes down. You are finally on the inside. And what's the first thing you do?

Complain.

"My book jacket looks like an Afterschool Special."

"The publisher put me on a *connecting flight!*"

"Mel passed, Russell passed, and now I can't put in my pool."

Writers are whiners, sufferers. Oddly, success only amplifies the moaning. Pre-success, when you're *really* suffering—oh, say, doing temp word processing eight hours a day, fighting your way home on an airless bus, slurping down a take-out burrito, and still, somehow, at the expense of all social interaction, forcing yourself to write—you don't have *time* to complain. Or think much. It's do or die.

It's later, in the gigantic house, gazing out over your acre of lawn, that the dissatisfaction starts. You've got what you wanted: control of your time. Control of your time, to a writer, means sitting by yourself in a room all day. Living largely inside your head, little slights, the slings and arrows that were, before, just shrugged off, now loom large. An unreturned call? Tragedy, tantrum. The dry cleaner loses a button? Go to bed for three days.

Ask any screenwriter, and he will tell you that the lowliest plantation slave had a better life than he does. Screenwriters are regularly whupped by the spiky egos of the famous, their premiere tickets limited to two (back of the bus!), their seven-figure incomes savaged by greedy ex-wives. It's enough to make you weep.

Is the answer then, to remain unproduced, anonymous—and on the planet? Of course not. The answer is to become a producer or director. Then you can complain about writers.

 Among **Leslie Dixon's** *many screen credits, nearly all major hits, are* Outrageous Fortune, The Thomas Crown Affair, *and* Mrs. Doubtfire.

54

Gentlemen,

Well, another day has gone by and you still haven't come to pick up my novel for publication.

Just for that, I am going to offer it to another publisher.

Nyahh! Nyahh! Nyahh!

Gentlemen, I am submitting a story to your magazine for consideration.

I have been a subscriber to your magazine for many years.

If you don't publish my story, I am going to cancel my subscription.

So there, too!

55

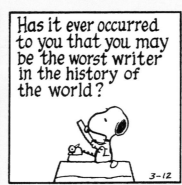

Oakley Hall

Maybe Snoopy is on the unfriendly end of so many rejection letters because he hasn't learned to lie well enough.

Storytelling is an elaborate form of lying. Both *fiction* and *story* are euphemisms for lies. It is the concern of us liars to give our falsehoods the semblance of truth, and a storyteller uses every device at his command to instill in his fiction the verisimilitude that convinces the reader.

I began trying to write fiction as the Adjutant of an Amphibian Tank Battalion stationed on the island of Maui, preparing for the invasion of Japan. I had been reading Raymond Chandler and Dashiell Hammett and trying to plot stories that might be published in *Black Mask* magazine, but with time on my hands, I got into Ernest Hemingway, and, later, William Faulkner, from the post library. Horizons expanded. Ambitions changed. How did they do it? There were no other would-be fiction writers I knew to talk to. I dimly understood that Hemingway left everything out but the essentials, while Faulkner jammed in so much that his novels were enor-

her...   stormy knight.

It was a dark
and st
Christmas

anwhile, on   il farm in
sas,   rowing up.
End of Part I

climbed into
arriage, he
d goodbye.

"How can I take you
anyplace when it's a
dark and stormy night?"
he said.

Call me
Ishmael.

ddenly, their dog, Rex,
ecided he'd better
ke over!

rent,"

It was a dark
and stormy night

le also said,
ave a nice day!"

By Supper
eir eyes met...   Possessed
e minutes later
y were married.

a crowded
e was lonely

mously rich. I was learning that good reading was the route to writing. But how did you even start, sitting alone in your tent with a typewriter propped up on an ammunition case?

More and more these days writers are communalized; in college writing programs, in local writing groups, in evening writing classes and summer writers conferences. But in the end this craft and sullen art is a solitary one. The writer confronts his typewriter or word processor, stares out his window, and cudgels his brain for inspiration.

My first teacher was Caroline Gordon, a southern novelist and short story writer of considerable reputation and strong opinions, who taught at Columbia University, which I attended on the GI Bill. She had sat at the knee of Ford Madox Ford, who had been a pupil of Henry James, which gave me a rather direct line to the Master.

Gordon worked from rules of writing established by James and Flaubert but also had many of her own devising. Sentences could only properly begin with certain words (I have forgotten which these were). In making fiction "come to life" usually two sensory details were necessary, although sometimes a particularly felicitous one would be sufficiently vivid. If more than two were called for, the writer should bear down on Selection, from the Jamesian dictum of Select, Contemplate, Render. In dialogue the writer should beware of employing more than two sentences per line, so that the line did not become a "speech." The names of principal characters and titles should contain long vowel sounds, with shorter vowel sounds for the names of lesser characters.

As a beginner I found it comforting to be governed by a set of rules, and I was happy under Gordon's dictatorship, especially as the two novels I completed at Columbia, the first a mystery and the second a mainstream, were published. Later, as I began to question her rules, I found that they had established themselves in my technique so strongly that it was difficult for me to flout them. I still am uncomfortable employing anything but a strict point of view, even though I have come to realize that in fiction, as in life, what works, works.

Clover Adams said of Henry James that he chewed more than he bit off. And in my readings, too, I had felt that in James there was sometimes more art than red meat. At Gordon's knee I had imbibed the lessons from James and Flaubert that everything in a novel—plot, character and action, scene, setting, and narrative—should mesh together like the gears of a watch. However, my second novel, *Corpus of Joe Bailey*, which was a best-seller and received a good deal of critical attention as well, was a messy, sprawling novel of growing up, with plenty of red meat to it. Gordon wrote, expressing sadness at my betrayal of her standards in going the "naturalistic" rather than the "classic" route. Her letter was, in fact, a severance of relations. I was feeling my oats by then and did not think that I had been justly rebuked.

I saw her again years later, by sheer chance, at a hacienda in Mexico where both of us happened to be guests. She was quite old. By now I had published almost as many novels as she had, but I immediately fell into my old teacher-pupil subordination. "What is your newest novel called, Oakley?" she asked me. When I replied that it was *Report From Beau Harbor*, she nodded approvingly. "That is a good title. The long vowel sounds convey to the reader the fact that it is a novel of serious intent."

Novels of serious intent are what I write. Probably novels that are not of serious intent are constructed and written in pretty much the same way, with the same necessities to be provided for. Indeed, it may be that a novel that is not of serious intent is a contradiction in terms. The task of putting seventy thousand and more words down on paper coherently, with a beginning, a middle, and an end, is such an overwhelming task that "serious" seems inadequate to describe it.

 Oakley Hall *is the author of twenty novels, including* Corpus of Joe Bailey, Apaches, *and* The Downhill Racers. *His novel* Warlock *was nominated for a Pulitzer Prize.*

61

It was a dark
and stormy
Christmas night.

62

Catherine Ryan
Hyde

Yeah. What is it with editors, anyway?

They send form rejections. They don't deign to comment. Or they scribble a mortal wound of an insult. Or you hear nothing for nine months. Or your story disappears entirely.

Who are these people? *Don't they appreciate what we go through?*

Years ago, I worked as an editorial assistant for a small literary journal. Do writers appreciate what an editor goes through?

Picture this: The "slush pile" is taller than me. Half the submissions are from people who know little about their marketplace. Their stories belong in *Field & Stream* or *Cat Fancy*, not a journal that publishes only fiction. Most are awash with typos and punctuation errors. Often they arrive with no personalized cover letter—just a small strip of paper with a few credits. I am to take half an hour of my life to read the submission. The author apparently wouldn't take five minutes to compose a letter addressing it to me.

I'm careful not to say anything kind, lest I receive a furious note that reads, "If you like it so much, why won't you publish it?"

Let me give you a few possible reasons.

We already have too many first-person stories for this issue. We ran a story about a dog last season. The Big Cheese editor is going through a messy divorce. Your story on divorce was swell. I don't want to show it to him. Do you?

Or, more likely, I've narrowed it down to six stories. And I have room for four. End of story.

There is an element of good fortune involved in getting your story to the right editor on the right day. Learn your market well, and accept that your odds are better here than in the lottery—but not by much.

Buy a lot of tickets, Snoopy.

There is an element of good fortune involved in getting your story to the right editor on the right day. Learn your market well, and accept that your odds are better here than in the lottery—but not by much.

Catherine Ryan Hyde *is the author of the novels* Funerals for Horses, Pay It Forward, Electric God, Walter's Purple Heart, *and the story collection* Earthquake Weather.

PEANUTS

Our magazine assumes no responsibility for unsolicited material.

No such material will be returned unless submitted with a self-addressed envelope and sufficient postage.

5-2

THEY PROBABLY DON'T REALLY MEAN IT!

U.S. MAIL

PEANUTS

"DEAR CONTRIBUTOR, YOUR STORY WAS TERRIBLE!"

"WE WOULD LIKE TO SEND IT BACK TO YOU, BUT YOU DID NOT INCLUDE RETURN POSTAGE"

" P.S. DON'T SEND THE RETURN POSTAGE NOW... "

4-3

" WE THREW YOUR STORY OUT THE WINDOW! "

65

66

YOUR WRITING IS TOO SIMPLE...

YOU NEED TO USE FANCY WORDS LIKE "UNBEKNOWNST"

Unbeknownst to everyone, it was a dark and stormy night.

© 1987 United Feature Syndicate, Inc.   7-1

SCHULZ

Fannie Flagg

"I'm not smart enough to be a writer," I said to myself, and probably to the person sitting next to me, as I slouched in my seat in the back row of the Santa Barbara Writer's Conference that first night. All my life I had secretly longed to be a writer, to pen a novel, as they say, but the fact that I was dyslexic and could not spell, had failed English, and did not have a college degree (barely got out of high school), somehow gave me the idea that for me to ever become a real writer was about as likely as a one-legged man becoming a tap dancer.

That year, 1975, when I snuck into the writers conference, feeling so inadequate and stupid, I remember looking around the room and thinking that the hundreds of people in the room that night were most likely all brilliant English professors with a vocabulary of more than 598 million words, and they not only knew them but could spell them, and I was sure most could even diagram a sentence and type sixty-seven thousand words a minute. I had barely mastered the ballpoint pen much less a typewriter.

But despite all these handicaps, I still wanted to write.

And, to my eternal surprise, at the end of that week I discovered that writing is not about degrees or vocabulary or diagramming a sentence. It is simply about the desire to tell a story. Lucy, you really don't need to use fancy words like "unbeknownst" or even know how to spell it to become a writer! The joy about writing is that as long as you write from your heart, a thousand English degrees cannot compete with that. And remember, an editor can always correct your spelling and fix your grammar, but only you can tell your story.

And, oh, by the way . . . there *was* a one-legged tap dancer named "Peg Leg Bates," and he made quite a good living.

His picture hangs over my desk.

Fannie Flagg *is the author of* Coming Attractions, Fried Green Tomatoes at the Whistle Stop Café, *and* Welcome to the World, Baby Girl!

> The joy about writing is that as long as you write from your heart, a thousand English degrees cannot compete with that.

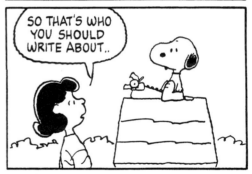

70

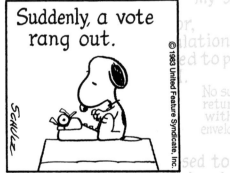

72

John Leggett

Snoopy, like so many beginning writers, appears to be overly concerned with setting, especially with nights that may or may not be dark and stormy. In the old, old days of leisurely read fiction, whole pages might be devoted to setting and weather. Not so today.

It is surely possible to tell a good story with no scene, no setting at all, no indication of where we are, just as we might expect to enjoy a play presented on a bare stage. If the characters and narrative are strong enough, they will hold our interest without any background.

But of course all events occur somewhere, and often the place where they occur has a profound influence over what occurs. The landscape of a story, its atmosphere, its feeling of harshness or mildness, of gloom or cheer, of beauty or ugliness, is likely to affect the characters and the way they lead their lives.

Setting would be critical to a story about a prisoner or to one about castaways adrift in the Pacific Ocean and very likely to one about a high-school graduation in an Appalachian coal town.

A story's setting is what puts us there, gives us readers a sense of being in the situation with the characters. If it is set in Honduras, we should feel hot, sweaty, and thirsty. We should see the sun baking the town square and the steam rising from the back of the little burro tethered at the side of the church. We should smell the *zozo*, the native delicacy of fish heads and banana skins, as it sizzles over the charcoal.

A setting, deftly portrayed, not only tells us where we are but gives the story a sense of truth, the credibility we speak of as verisimilitude. It does wonders for that troublesome disbelief and the reader's willing suspension thereof.

Deft portrayal of setting is a matter of selectivity, of choosing only a few details and letting the reader supply the rest. We readers come to a story with plenty of scenic equipment and become restive if prevented from using it by a storyteller who paints the whole set for us and lists the furniture and the contents of the drawers as if we were tenants to be held accountable.

People whose lives are affected by fiction, who live with one foot in the real and the other in a fictional world, tend to store up their scenic memory without differentiating between the two.

A story's setting is what puts us there, gives us readers a sense of being in the situation with the characters. If it is set in Honduras, we should feel hot, sweaty, and thirsty. We should see the sun baking the town square and the steam rising from the back of the little burro tethered at the side of the church.

That, it seems to me, is one of the particular enrichments of reading and writing stories. We don't see the dreary little Southern community and its poverty-stricken surroundings that appear before us. Rather, we see Yoknapatawpha County and wonder if that could be Flem Snopes there on the porch, with his hat down over his eyes.

But the real purpose of scene is its contribution to the story's total, emotional effect. If it isn't adding to that, the scene will be a distraction from, and a detraction to, the story.

An autumnal setting can add a sense of ending and loss to a story about a doomed love, just as a spring setting can add a sense of anticipation to a story about adolescence. Setting can be put to ironic use, too, so that the springtime setting could add poignancy to a story about death.

So, Snoopy, we'll let you tell us whether the night was stormy or maybe dark or balmy or springlike or threatening or rainy, but then for heaven's sake, get on with your story!

 John Leggett *is the author of many books, including the classic* Ross and Tom, *plus the definitive biography of William Saroyan.*

76

onely.　He was a dark and
her...　　stormy knight.

It was a dark
　and stormy
Christmas night.

...anwhile, on a sm...
...nsas, a boy was g...
　End of Part I

...e climbed into
...arriage, he
...d goodbye.

Call me
　Ishmael.

"How can I take you
anyplace when it's a
dark and stormy night?"
he...

...uddenly, their do...
...ecided he'd be...
...ke over!

...rent,"
...ll

...He also said,
...ave a nice day!"

By Supper
...heir eyes met... Possessed
...ve minutes later
...ey were married.

...s a crowded

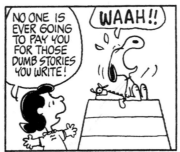

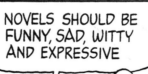

Dominick Dunne

How I empathize with Snoopy! Lucy must have written that review of my first book for *The New York Times* so many years ago.

I'm a late-life writer—I didn't *start* writing until I was fifty years old. So take heart some of you! When I graduated from Williams College, the first job I had was stage manager of the *Howdy Doody Show*. From there I went to some of the great live television shows of that period. Then I produced a lot of movies, *The Boys in the Band, Panic in Needle Park, Play It As It Lays,* and so forth. Exciting times, but I had the feeling this wasn't *it*. I got more and more discontented.

Finally, I walked away from Hollywood, and I went to Oregon, a cabin in the woods, and began to write my first novel. You know, it's one thing to say you're going to write a novel and it sounds so great when you tell your friends about this wonderful Hollywood scandal you're going to write about, and they say, "Oh, that's fabulous," but then you get there in the cabin all by yourself and you go to the typewriter, and it never sounds the same way when you get it down on paper—*if* you get it down on paper. And if any of you are having that problem I want to tell you what you have to do: Set a certain time each day to be your writing time, and nothing—*nothing*—must interfere with that time. *That Is Your Writing Time*, in capital letters.

I worked hard on that book. It was based on a true case about a famous Hollywood producer who stole some money from an actor, and it got published and it was such a flop, a real bomb. It was called *The Winners*. And it got the worst review imaginable in *The New York Times*; they just savaged it.

I've always been very sensitive, and I'd worked hard on that book—it's just as hard to write a bad book as a good one, you know. But let me tell you how I took that terrible criticism.

I told myself, "Listen, I'm fifty-three years old and I wrote a book and I got a book published by Simon and Schuster and by god it got reviewed in *The New York Times*!"

So I didn't give up, and Michael Korda, the editor, believed in me, and he said, "Listen, Dominick, you know all these fancy people, and there's nothing that the public likes to read more than about the rich and the powerful in a criminal situation." And let me tell you, I heard those words and a bell went off! I thought, *That's it!*

You see, I'd seen this famous showgirl in the Stork Club one night—she was married to this guy from one of the most prominent Long Island families. She was just a knockout, this lady, and they got up to dance, and when she stood up—she was in a strapless evening dress, and in the fifties when ladies wore strapless dresses they had one of the great gestures of all times—and that was when they did *this* on one side and they did *this* on the other side. And I was just dazzled by

...it's one thing to say you're going to write a novel and it sounds so great when you tell your friends about this wonderful Hollywood scandal you're going to write about, and they say, "Oh, that's fabulous," but then you get there in the cabin all by yourself and you go to the typewriter, and it never sounds the same way when you get it down on paper ...

this woman, and when she walked out to the dance floor it was like "Out of my way, everybody!" She started to dance with this man and she had her lips right at his ear and she sang to him the whole time, and I said this is *it*, this is how I want to live! I want to be with these people like this always! A year later she shot and killed that man. I told the story to Korda, and he said, "That's the novel you're going to write."

And that's how *The Two Mrs. Grenvilles* came into being.

So, Snoopy, just ignore Lucy's comments—or anyone else's—and keep on writing!

Dominick Dunne *has written five best-selling novels, produced major films, and has written several hundred magazine articles. His latest novel, A Solo Act, is on its way.*

83

84

It

PEANUTS®

Schulz

"IT"... YES, I LIKE THAT

It was a dark and stormy night.

"YOU NEVER TAKE ME ANYPLACE,'SHE COMPLAINED"

"How can I take you anyplace when it's a dark and stormy night?" he said.

" THEIR MARRIAGE WAS RAPIDLY COMING APART"

5-7

© 1989 United Feature Syndicate, Inc.

They were behind with their car payments, and the rent on the condominium was due.

WHAT A SAD LITTLE STORY..

I'LL BE ANXIOUS TO SEE HOW YOU GET THEM OUT OF THEIR TROUBLES..

Suddenly, their dog, Rex, decided he'd better take over!

Schulz

86

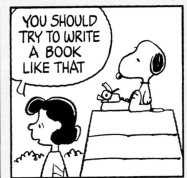

William F. Buckley, Jr.

Snoopy: You will at one point need to decide how to deal with your critics. My friend David Niven, whose three books were runaway best-sellers, told me that he made it a point to write to *every* book critic. That was a tall assignment because (1) everybody reviewed *The Moon's a Balloon* and *Bring On the Empty Horses*, and (2) all the reviews were favorable. Nobody ever disparaged anything David Niven ever did. The problem became: What do you say to the one hundredth favorable critic?

It's easier to write to someone who gives you a negative review, being a greater bite in the situation; and then strange relationships can ensue.

I wrote a very negative review of *By Love Possessed* (which *The New York Times Magazine* labeled *By Sex Obsessed*), but in it I remarked that the hostility to the novel by critic Dwight

It's easier to write to someone who gives you a negative review, being a greater bite in the situation; and then strange relationships can ensue.

Macdonald, in his famous review in *The New Yorker*, was overdone. So, I get a letter from James Gould Cozzens. It is animated by sheer *hatred* of Dwight Macdonald and gratitude to me for going after him.

I think that was one of maybe a dozen letters I had from Cozzens. I thought myself such a friend, at one point, I volunteered to make time to meet him at Williamstown when I was there lecturing. He instantly turned on the freeze button—he could write letters but didn't encourage any intrusion in his eremitical life.

So, don't be superstitious either about the need to write to a favorable critic, *or* a negative critic. I rather like the occasional letter I get from book authors whose work I review. And sometimes a reviewer will have taken such manifest pains to read your book carefully, and generously, you'll want to tell him (him/her!) you appreciated what . . . *they (!)* . . . did.

Which reminds me, Snoopy, don't try to write a book like J.G. Cozzens. He became too long-winded, besides which the rule is: Don't try to write like J.G. Cozzens unless you can.

Good luck!

Since God and Man at Yale, **William F. Buckley, Jr.** *has written dozens of books, both fiction and nonfiction, most of them best-sellers.*

88

David Michaelis

One of the central ideas in *Peanuts* is that you are who you are—you're stuck with yourself. Snoopy may never be the novelist he wants to be, and he will surely struggle as a biographer. To do the biographer's job—to chart the emotional evolution of a human being, to tell the story of how a person becomes him or herself—Snoopy will first have to see *himself* as he really is. Having recognized the reality of his own fancies and evasions, having shed his most cherished illusions, Snoopy will be capable of seeing clearly into the conflicts of his subject's character, and, in so doing, come face to face with uncertainties, mysteries, and doubts about himself.

"Pick out some person you like," advises Linus, playing directly into Snoopy's worst fear about himself and others. Whatever else Snoopy thinks he is, or wants to be, he's human enough to know this much that's unlikeable about himself: "We dogs don't like anyone." The truth is, Snoopy *can't* interest himself in a life other than his own because he's still torn between his true

Whatever conceit first divides the biographer from his subject—temperament, taste, even the implacable partition of death itself—can in the end be bridged only by a seasoned, unbiased love.

nature and the wider range of his ambitions. Liking someone else "might be kind of hard." For although the biographer may start by picking someone likeable, there will surely come a time when he shakes his head in wondrous disgust that he could ever have paired himself with such a person. Whatever conceit first divides the biographer from his subject—temperament, taste, even the implacable partition of death itself—can in the end be bridged only by a seasoned, unbiased love.

If Snoopy is to be capable of biography, he will not only have to accumulate facts but account for truths—his own and another's. And, as John Keats would remind him, with the unflinching precision of a twentieth-century poet like Linus Van Pelt: "A fact is not a truth until you love it."

David Michaelis *is writing the first full-length biography of Charles M. Schulz. He is the author of the best-selling* N.C. Wyeth: A Biography.

her...   stormy knight.

It was a dark and stormy Christmas night.

...anwhile...arm in ...sas, a boy was growing up.

End of Part I

...e climbed into ...arriage, he ...ed goodbye.

"How can I take you anyplace when it's a dark and stormy night?" he said.

Call me Ishmael.

...ddenly, their dog, Rex, ...ecided he'd better ...ke over!

...rent,"

It was a dark and stormy night

He also said, ...ave a nice day!"

By Supper ...eir eyes met... Possessed ...ve minutes later ...ey were married.

...a crowded ...e was lonely.

92

PEANUTS

Helen Sweetstory was born on a small farm on April 5, 1950.

I THINK I'LL SKIP ALL THE STUFF ABOUT HER PARENTS AND GRANDPARENTS...THAT'S ALWAYS KIND OF BORING...

2-25

I'LL ALSO SKIP ALL THE STUFF ABOUT HER STUPID CHILDHOOD... I'LL GO RIGHT TO WHERE THE ACTION BEGAN...

It was raining the night of her high-school prom.

SCHULZ

PEANUTS

I THINK I'LL SEND MISS HELEN SWEETSTORY A COPY OF MY MANUSCRIPT, "IT WAS A DARK AND STORMY NIGHT"

FAMOUS AUTHORS LIKE TO RECEIVE MANUSCRIPTS FROM UNKNOWN WRITERS..

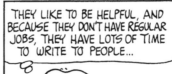

THEY LIKE TO BE HELPFUL, AND BECAUSE THEY DON'T HAVE REGULAR JOBS, THEY HAVE LOTS OF TIME TO WRITE TO PEOPLE...

4-20

BESIDES, MISS SWEETSTORY LOVES ME!

SCHULZ

Her love affair had ended. She didn't want to live.	She threw herself in front of a Zamboni.	THAT'S THE DUMBEST THING I'VE EVER READ!

She threw herself in front of a skateboard.

Travel Tips... "Arriving Home"

When putting away your luggage after arriving home, always close the zippers so bugs can't crawl in.

THAT'S THE DUMBEST TRAVEL TIP I'VE EVER READ!

IT'S NOT SO BAD WHEN YOU CONSIDER I'VE NEVER BEEN ANYWHERE...

Frances Weaver

Like Snoopy, how do we writers know what's funny or isn't? In real life if we tell a story and people laugh, we know it's funny.

But in print?

And just what is humor anyway? Certainly surprise is an important element.

Charles Chaplin defined "comic surprise" in these terms: The ugly villain is chasing the beautiful heroine down the street. We see on the sidewalk a banana peel. The camera cuts back and forth from the banana peel to the approaching villain. We know what's going to happen. Or do we? At the very last second the bad guy sees the banana peel and jumps over it—and falls into an open manhole. Surprise!

Humor, as Charles Schulz proved every day, doesn't have to be of the slapstick variety; his humor came from the small funny things of life.

My humor writing stems from everyday observations and my own unexpected family experiences—some funny, some not so funny, and some a combination of the two, like the following example.

Our son Ross had turned eight when the youngest, Matt, came along. Having a baby brother did not excite Ross much. One summer day I laid the new baby on the couch in the living room, instructing Ross to "watch the baby" while I collected my purse and the paraphernalia to take Matt to the doctor's for his six-month checkup. Matt promptly rolled off the couch, striking his head on the foot of the coffee table. Result: a depressed fracture of his soft little skull.

Surgery on the head occupied most of the rest of our summer, but Matt recovered in good shape.

Months later, in the dark dead of winter, Ross made several evening trips through the kitchen into the backyard; alone. This generally happened while I was cleaning up after dinner. All by himself, this nine-year-old meandered out in the cold dark evening. Curiosity got the best of me.

"Ross, why are you going out there? Don't you need a coat? Are you checking on the dogs? They're okay. Why do you go out in the dark alone?"

"I don't want to tell you, Mother."

"Oh, come on, now, Ross. You can tell me. What's the matter?"

"I just can't tell you, Mom."

A little more urging brought this embarrassed reply: "Mother, I've been going out in the yard to pray." Eyes to the floor.

"Pray?! You've been out there praying? Why, Honey?"

Shifting feet, still no eye contact. "Well, Mother, I've been praying for God to forgive me because I let my baby brother roll off and hit his head so he had to have an operation."

I gasped. "Oh, darling! How sweet! It wasn't all your fault. They baby's gonna be all right. How dear of you. I'm sure God forgives you!"

Caught up in the sweetness of the moment with that blessed boy, I impulsively hugged him. A big bear hug. *He reeked of cigar smoke.*

"Ross!! You haven't been praying. You've been smoking! What the . . . ?"

He shook himself free of the hug and stood there shaking his head. "No."

I insisted. He denied. That went on for a few minutes. Finally Ross admitted: "I did not smoke. I tried to smoke, but I couldn't get Dad's cigars to stay lighted."

Well, at least he had *thought* about praying.

Sigmund Freud wrote, "The most favorable condition for comic pleasure is a generally happy disposition in which one is in the mood for laughter. In happy toxic states almost everything seems comic. We laugh at the expectation of laughing, at the appearance of one who is presenting the comic material (sometimes even before he attempts to make us laugh), and finally, we laugh at the recollection of having laughed."

Siggy would have liked Snoopy a lot.

Frances Weaver *is the author of* The Girls With the Grandmother Faces, I'm Not As Old As I Used to Be, *and* Runaway Grandma.

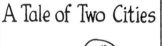 A Tale of Two Cities

REALLY?

Of Human Bondage

7-30

YOU'RE KIDDING!

Heart of Darkness

I CAN'T BELIEVE IT!!

I HAVE A GREAT IDEA FOR A NOVEL, BUT ALL THE GOOD TITLES ARE TAKEN!

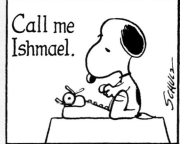

Herbert Gold

"Your novel starts too slowly…You need a more powerful beginning" reminds me, with a pang and a stomachache, of the lessons about endings inadvertently taught to me by my twin sons, aged fourteen, and at another time, by a young Danish woman on the train from Paris to Copenhagen.

First, my sons. I was obsessively piling up sheets of paragraphs, plans, projects, preliminaries for the last chapter of a novel, *A Girl of Forty*. Somehow I was reluctant to end the story, and reluctance was translated into scribbled notes—notes, notes, and more notes. During this period of struggle, my sons decided to earn an allowance by cleaning my studio. They dusted, they swatted flies, they shot rubber bands out the window, and one day they trashed the unruly pile of paper by my desk. Instead of reproaching them, I threw up.

The next morning, I went to the typewriter with desperation in my heart and rewrote the last chapter. I was loose and sweaty. Some of the brilliant ideas and poignant phrases I had been

103

The next morning, I went to the typewriter with desperation in my heart and rewrote the last chapter. I was loose and sweaty.

stocking may have fueled the effort, but I couldn't remember them, so I merely plunged in and brought the story home.

I still adored my sons, but I advised them in the future to kill flies rather than devote themselves to the editing process.

Another time, another book; brooding over another last chapter. I decided to break free of all familiar distractions with only my notebook and a pen for company, but the blessed spirit of Hans Christian Anderson had something else in mind for me. On the Paris-Copenhagen train, a Danish person expressed interest in my stumbling effort to speak Danish. Tongue-tied in the presence of her Danish beauty and charm, I carried her bag off the train. I then suggested dinner at Do Kanten, which means "Two Fountains." She accepted the invitation. I left on the train the notebook in which I had written the last chapter of *Mister White Eyes*.

Same results: nausea, despair, open pores, and then a rapid sprint to put things together. In both cases, the preparation in brooding and the passion of letting go improved the rhythm of the novels. At least, that's my opinion, and who else should judge? So my sons and the young Danish woman were blessings in different ways; nature in its goodness provides us with a bounty of alternative blessings.

Herbert Gold *is the author of the best-sellers* The Man Who Was Not With It, Salt, *and* Fathers, *among many others, plus dozens of short stories.*

YOU SHOULD WRITE A SENTIMENTAL CHRISTMAS STORY..

IT SHOULD BE SAD, BUT VERY INSPIRING...

11-27

IT ALSO SHOULD HAVE A CHARACTER IN IT THAT EVERYONE WILL LOVE

"Tiny Jim"

© 1982 United Feature Syndicate, Inc.

THIS IS THE HOLIDAY SEASON

IF YOU WERE SMART, YOU'D WRITE A NICE CHRISTMAS STORY...

11-26

© 1982 United Feature Syndicate, Inc.

It was a dark and stormy Christmas night.

106

Sue Grafton

Poor Snoopy! It's hard to tell if he's taken Lucy's suggestion, or if, on reflection, he's decided to stick with his original choice. You'll find that *everyone* has an opinion about your story and what you should do with it. Start with a slam-bang opening. Switch the first two chapters so that the book begins with chapter two and then loops back to chapter one. Cut the flashbacks. Create a backstory. Forget the romance. Add a love interest. More jeopardy! No, less! Too much exposition. Not enough . . .

One of the most difficult decisions an unpublished writer makes is when to take advice and when to ignore all your well-meaning critics and do it your way. (Almost) every work of fiction can bear improvement. When you're first starting out, it's hard to know how much is enough and how much is too much, where you've engaged your reader and where you've bored her to tears. It's tempting to submit your manuscript to everyone you know: friends and relatives, co-workers, classmates, members of your critique group. It's natural to want feedback—some sense of how you're doing so you'll know what to do next.

While I'm as opinionated as the next guy (though, of course, I'm right more often than anyone else), I still believe it's your job as a writer to make these judgments yourself. Write long enough and you'll know the good sentences from the clunkers. Complete twenty-five short stories, and you'll figure out which ones work and which don't. Read your dialogue aloud, and you'll soon be able to distinguish the lines that sound "real" from those that sound stilted or phony.

Writing is self-taught. Most of us learn to write well by writing badly for a long, long time. What's deceptive is that early in the process *everything* you write sounds terrific to you. You're convinced you've done a great job, that your story is compelling, that your characters are complex and well-developed. It's only later, rereading, when your initial passion for the piece has passed, that you realize where you've fallen short. Sometimes a rewrite is the remedy. Sometimes a manuscript is best relegated to the bottom drawer. The point is, your job as a writer is to learn from yourself, to identify your own mistakes and find ways to correct them so that next time around, you can take another step toward honing your skills. Consulting other people only teaches you to depend on their reactions, which may or may not be legitimate. Quit looking for approval. Quit seeking advice. Learn to evaluate your own work with a dispassionate eye. This way, the lessons you acquire will be all the more valuable because you've mastered your craft from within.

> One of the most difficult decisions an unpublished writer makes is when to take advice and when to ignore all your well-meaning critics and do it your way.

Sue Grafton's *unique alphabetical series starring detective Kinsey Millhone and beginning with* A is for Alibi *is a publishing legend.*

Jay Conrad Levinson

To me, writing a book is a two-part process. The first part, and probably the toughest, is starting the book. That part, when complete, is only one line or one paragraph long. I try to get a little more down on the page than Snoopy but not a whole lot more.

The second part, which I've always considered much easier, is completing the book. It's much longer than starting, but also considerably easier—because now, momentum is on my side. It's kind of like jumping out of an airplane. The first step is nearly brutal, but the rest is just a matter of going with gravity.

The way I write a book, and this may seem demented to others, is first to organize what I have to say by dividing the information into ten parts. Ten seems to be my magic number or lucky number. It's the starting point for any book I author.

Next comes the research, an ongoing process. Most of it I've already gleaned. The rest comes from being passionate about my topic and searching every nook and cranny of bookstores, the Internet, and peoples' minds for more information to fill the empty spaces. Sometimes, there's so much that I'm forced to write a twelve- or twenty-chapter book. No problem, because regardless of how many chapters there are, they're all merely an aspect of the second part of my writing process.

It's the act of writing that I love the most. I go into a state of flow that's always easy to achieve. I lose track of time and feel, deep in my heart, that God is flowing through me. I'm such a fast typist that God has to hustle to keep up. I edit as I write—each line, paragraph, chapter. That means most of my books are completed in one draft.

It's the act of writing that I love the most.

The best advice I can offer is to skip writing if you don't love to write.

Jay Conrad Levinson *is the author of the* Guerrilla Marketing *books, nineteen in all, including* Guerrilla Marketing for Writers.

113

114

She called him "cute"

PEANUTS.
by SCHULZ

She called him "adorable,"

and it caused him more trouble than anything that ever happened to him in his whole life.

"adorable" HMM..

THAT'S A PRETTY GOOD BEGINNING..

4-6

A GOOD BEGINNING IS VERY IMPORTANT..

I LIKE A GOOD BEGINNING..

THIS ISN'T THE BEGINNING.. THIS IS THE ENDING!

SCHULZ

Barnaby Conrad

Lucy is so right, and Snoopy better pay attention! Remember, when an editor takes your piece out of its manila envelope, you will not be there at his elbow to say, "Keep reading! It gets really good later on—terrific scene coming up!"

There'll be no "later on" if the editor is not intrigued right off the bat. He does not necessarily have to be shocked, startled, or amazed, but the editor, putting himself in the place of a reader, must be tantalized enough to read further. A well-crafted opening immediately tells the editor that he is dealing with a good writer; professional writers seldom write a dull first page of a novel or short story. Therefore, as you sit down to start to write, consider these suggestions and options:

1   Try to pick the most intriguing place in your piece to begin.

2   Try to create attention-grabbing images of a setting if that's where you want to begin.

3   Raise the reader's curiosity about what is happening or is going to happen in an action scene.

4   Describe a character so compellingly that we want to learn more about what happens to him or her.

5   Present a situation so vital to our protagonist that we must read on.

...ely, he was a dark and
er... stormy knight.

It was a dark, and stormy christmas night.

nwhile, a small farm in
sas, a boy was growing up.
End of Part I

climbed into
rriage, he
goodbye.

Call me
Ishmael.

"How can I take you
anyplace when it's a
dark and stormy night?"
he said.

ddenly, their dog, Rex,
cided he'd better
e over!

ent,"

It was a dark
and stormy night

e also said,
ve a nice day!"

By Supper
Possessed

ir eyes met...
e minutes later
were married.

a crowded

6 And most important, no matter what method you choose, *start with something happening!* (And not with rumination. A character sitting in a cave or in jail or in a kitchen or in a car ruminating about the meaning of life and how he got to this point does not constitute *something happening*.)

...no matter what method you choose, start with something happening!

Hone your opening words, for just as stories aren't written but rewritten, so should beginnings be written and rewritten. Look at your opening and ask yourself, "If I were reading this, would I be intrigued enough to go on?"

And remember: Always aim for the heart!

An O. Henry Prize short story winner, **Barnaby Conrad** *has authored thirty books, including* Matador, Hemingway's Spain, The Complete Guide to Writing Fiction, *and* Name Dropping, *the story of his San Francisco saloon. He wrote a Playhouse 90 for John Frankenheimer, the screenplay for John Steinbeck's* Flight, *and a Broadway play based on his novel* Dangerfield.

121

Elizabeth George

If you decide on a life of crime—crime writing, that is—you have to come to terms with the fact that everyone is a critic, and everyone has at least two cents to put into your process. Witness poor Snoopy. There he is, meditating on the shape his timeless prose shall take and in comes Linus, proposing a Maguffin. Wily Snoopy, who is nobody's fool, chooses the most timeless Maguffin of them all and puts a little English on it, spinning it to reflect his interpretation of this particular writing technique.

But what to do when your friends, relatives, spouse, spousal equivalent, writing group members, potential agents, and strangers on the street give you advice about your writing? How do you determine whether what they have to say is actually legit? I think there's only one reasonable answer to these questions: Go within. You can spend your entire life writing and rewriting the same first chapter if you listen to other people's opinions and ignore the one sure place where you will always find the truth: in your own body.

I always tell my writing students to become completely aware of their bodies as they write. I tell them that their minds will lie to them all the time, but their guts will never lie to them. You know when you are afraid, don't you? You *feel* it; you don't think it. You know when you are excited, too. You know when you've done something that violates your personal code of honor and when you've done something that sustains your belief in your worth. You know these things because you feel them in your gut, and you have to learn to apply that gut reaction to your writing as well. When you are telling the story you are meant to tell, you are actually going to feel the truth of it, and in feeling that truth, your spirit is going to soar. When you are telling that story the way it needs to be told—through the kind of writing you can be proud of—you are going to feel that as well. If you become aware of that feeling of sureness, soundness, and wholeness that develops inside you when you are on the right track, then you won't be led astray by anyone else's opinion.

This doesn't mean that you listen to no one and think only that your writing is perfect, because it probably isn't. What it does mean is that you listen to what others say (choosing your critics judiciously), and when what they say has the ring of truth to it, you try it out and see how it feels inside when you do it. This could be something as simple as moving a scene from position A to position B in your book. It could be something more involved like a change in point of view. But in any case, when you do it, if you center yourself and become aware of how your body is reacting to what you're writing, you'll know you're heading in the right direction or the wrong direction through what your body tells you.

Sound strange? I'm sure it does if you haven't tried it or if you're the kind of person who exists mostly in her head, just like me. You might have to begin by listening to what your body tells you about situations having nothing whatsoever to do with your writing: like being in a crowded elevator, like being alone on a dark street at night, like being approached by a stranger.

123

If you acknowledge what your body tells you in these situations and others—rather than allowing your mind to talk you out of feeling what you're feeling—then you'll find you can ultimately apply your guts to your writing as well.

I've been writing this way for almost twenty years now. Like Snoopy, I never attended a writers conference (until I was published), and with the exception of two creative writing classes when I was nineteen, I'm almost entirely self-taught. When I've sought advice on or a reaction to a particular novel, I've sought it from a single individual per book, choosing someone who has no axe to grind and who reads fiction daily. I give that person the novel with two lists of questions that I want answered about the writing itself. One list is for her to look over before she begins the reading. The second list is in a sealed envelope for her to open after her reading. In this way I can direct the person to look for specific areas that I feel might be weak, or I can keep from influencing her thoughts about a novel by keeping her in the dark with regard to my questions till they're done. I never give a book to anyone and just say, "Tell me anything you want to tell me about it." I save that particular joy for my editor.

I think the writing life is the best life there is. It's also the most challenging. It's filled with a heck of a lot of difficult moments, but overcoming them is the most rewarding thing I've ever done.

You can spend your entire life writing and re-writing the same first chapter if you listen to other people's opinions and ignore the one sure place where you will always find the truth: in your own body.

Elizabeth George's *best-selling mysteries, such as* Well-Schooled in Murder, *are all set in England.*

124

stormy knight.

It was a dark
and stormy
Christmas night.

eanwhile, on a small farm in
nsas, a boy was growing up.

End of Part I

e climbed into
carriage, he
ed goodbye.

Call me
Ishmael.

"How can I take you
anyplace when it's a
dark and stormy night?"
he said.

uddenly, their dog, Rex,
decided he'd better
ake over!

erent."
ll

It was a dark
and stormy night

He also said,
Have a nice day!"

By Supper
heir eyes met...   Possessed
ve minutes later
ey were married.

s a crowded
He was lonely

NOT A BAD STORY

THIS ONE SECTION BOTHERS ME, THOUGH...

I THINK YOU SHOULD CROSS OUT THE PART WHERE YOUR HERO TAKES A NAP...

10-3

Z-Z-Z-Z-Z—

© 1985 United Feature Syndicate, Inc.

YES, MA'AM..DO YOU HAVE ANY BOOKS HERE IN YOUR LIBRARY WHERE A DOG TAKES OVER THE WHOLE WORLD?

© 1993 United Feature Syndicate, Inc.

WELL, I THINK NOW YOU'VE GOT ONE..

8-11

Budd Schulberg

Maybe Snoopy should just forget about being a great novelist and his obsession of outdoing Leo Tolstoy. Maybe he should start thinking shorter.

Short stories are great for a good night's reading, and on planes and trains—easier to read a short story than a novel in a subway. I don't only mean that a short story is short—a twenty-, thirty-minute read. A short story is also something you can reexperience, relive, reflect on—whatever you want to do with it—while waiting for your plane to be called or letting your watch warn you that your ferry from Orient Point is approaching New London. That would distract you from thinking about a novel, say *1984* or *Tender Is the Night*. But it gives you just enough time to ask yourself, Why did I like that story? Why did it hold me? What does it make me think about? Good stories are to enjoy. *Tell me a story, Daddy. Well, once upon a time* . . . Fun. But very good stories do more. First they entertain you, then they add to knowledge you already think you knew. They stretch you. Aesthetic aerobics.

A great blue heron just flew by my window. Where was it going, in the dead of winter? The germ of a story, or a tale. That's how they begin. Of course, a large bird flying by your window is simply a fact. An odd or interesting fact. A paragraph for *Audubon* magazine. What would make it a story? Well, if this large, pale blue bird is an anthropomorphic creature, he could be a symbol of a lost soul in a changing world. Why hasn't he gone south to the warmer climes that self-respecting blue herons expect and deserve? Is he a herald of the greenhouse effect: He thinks or senses that our winters are getting warmer? Is he a metaphor for climatic aberration leading to social alienation? Or could this be the story of a bird whose mate has been killed by man or some other marauder? Many birds, from racing pigeons to swans, mate for life. Will this one continue to search for his lost mate until he freezes or starves to death? Or will a human sympathizer get involved? Will he or she try to get to the bottom of this mystery of the great blue heron who chose to stay, or simply was left behind? How does the human character we've brought into the story cope with this problem? Do the intervention and the coping change it from a fleeting event to a story? The possibilities, we begin to see, are limitless. A story is not an event but a series of related events, one drawing on the previous one and building to a climax. It doesn't have to be a big payoff climax like a smoochy clinch or a screeching car chase at the end of a movie. It can be quiet and almost deceptively uneventful. Chekhov comes to mind as the master of such an ending and so does Hemingway, whose novels may date a little but whose short stories are still wonderful on rereading. Any student of the short story would do well to study their endings.

First the faces, then what Fitzgerald wisely equated with plot: characters in action; finally that good old beginning, middle, and end. And beyond the structure that holds it all together, there should be something more, the reason you're telling this tale. If characters-in-action equals plot, then plot-to-a-purpose equals theme. Take the theme away, and we're just out there juggling for the hell of it.

 Budd Schulberg *is the author of the classic* What Makes Sammy Run, The Disenchanted, On the Waterfront, *and* The Harder They Fall.

130

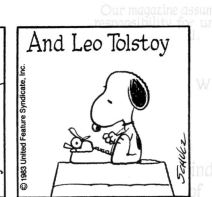

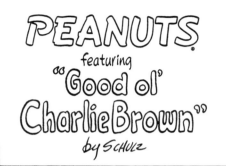

Monte Schulz

All things belonging to the earth will never change—the leaf, the blade, the flower, the wind that cries and sleeps and wakes again, the trees whose stiff arms clash and tremble in the dark, and the dust of lovers long since buried in the earth—all things proceeding from earth to seasons, all things that lapse and change and come again upon the earth—these things will always be the same, for they come up from the earth that never changes, they go back into the earth that lasts forever. Only the earth endures, but it endures forever.

—Thomas Wolfe, *You Can't Go Home Again*

Back in the 1930s, Bernard DeVoto addressed the legend of Thomas Wolfe by determining that "however useful genius may be in the writing of novels, it is not enough in itself—it has never been enough, in any art, and it never will be." Perhaps this is so. Certainly Wolfe did not write conventional novels. His books were never character studies, nor intricately plotted narratives. He was no paperback writer. His passion for words themselves was too great, his majestic vision of American life too vast to be captured and contained by structured fiction. Instead he poured out his heart in great torrents that described his own fury. He tried to describe the enormity of life in all its joy and bitterness, and legacy of language itself as art form in fiction. James Joyce did the same in *Ulysses* and *Finnegans Wake*, as did William Faulkner throughout his saga of Yokna-patawpha County, and, more recently, Cormac McCarthy in *Suttree*.

Words have a beauty unto themselves. The soaring aesthetic of Thomas Wolfe's language, his ear for colloquial rhythms, that flood of fury and passion, carried his narrative forward, gave its own shape and purpose to his novels, while transmuting the ordinary prose discourse of fictional prose into a fantastic poetry of compulsion and wanderlust for which he will always be remembered. It is easier to read Wolfe's novels and find fault in his leisurely plotting than to dismiss the sheer power of his artistic exuberance. Beautiful language can be as fascinating as clever storytelling. Poets know this. The clever play of words on the page can be like a rainbow splash of color on a painter's canvas. Style is more than a way of telling a tale. It's not only how a writer offers his or her narrative in the marketplace but how that writer feels about the written word, about language and how words ought to be used. And often we discover the authors we love best according to which words they use on a page and how they are arranged. Since Ernest Hemingway, it's been easy to dismiss and deride those writers like Thomas Wolfe ("And in woodland darkness great birds fluttered to their sleep—in sleeping woodlands strange and secret birds, the teal, the nightjar, and the flying rail went to their sleep with flutterings dark as hearts of sleeping men") and James Joyce ("Molly Bloom, fairhaired, greenvested, slimsandalled, her blue scarf in the seawind, simply swirling, breaks from the arms of her lover and calls, her young eyes wonderwide") whose artistry pours forth in streams of words poetic, alliterative, evocative. Isn't this, too, why we write? For the music of beautiful language? A celebration of words brings the writer to the page and the reader to the writer. Nor does it take a genius to appreciate this simple truth.

Monte Schulz *is the son of Charles M. Schulz. He has a master's degree in American Studies from the University of California at Santa Barbara and is the author of the novel* Down By The River. *He divides his time between Nevada City, California, and Santa Barbara, where he is finishing his second novel.*

THOMAS HARDY SAW A GIRL ON A BUS ONE DAY...

HE SAID SHE HAD "ONE OF THOSE FACES OF MARVELOUS BEAUTY WHICH ARE SEEN CASUALLY IN THE STREETS, BUT NEVER AMONG ONE'S FRIENDS"

"WHERE DO THEY COME FROM? WHO MARRIES THEM? WHO KNOWS THEM?" HE WONDERED

WHO CARES? AND WHO WAS THOMAS HARDY?

© 1982 United Feature Syndicate, Inc.

BONK!

"THOMAS HARDY ONCE SAW 'A HANDSOME MAID WITH LARGE INNOCENT EYES' RIDING IN A CART.. SHE WAS OBVIOUSLY VERY POOR.. WHICH MADE HARDY WONDER WHAT HER BEAUTY WOULD LEAD TO "

FOUR-WHEEL DRIVE PICKUP COMMERCIALS!

© 1988 United Feature Syndicate, Inc.

A. Scott Berg

You blockheads! Think what you will about Lucy: I say her taste in literature reveals a sensitive soul—a bold and ambitious romantic.

Until my second year at Princeton I had never read Thomas Wolfe; but when I announced to the distinguished biographer and teacher Carlos Baker that I wanted to write a biography of the legendary Scribner's editor Max Perkins, Professor Baker said, "I know you've read your Fitzgerald and Hemingway, but you can't possibly write about Perkins without having read Wolfe," his most challenging author.

Suddenly I thought of those thick thousand-page books my father had long tried to get me to read. Sigh. After a moment, I swallowed hard and strode to the library, where I checked out Wolfe's four massive novels. From the first words of *Look Homeward, Angel*—". . . a stone, a leaf, an unfound door"—I was hooked; and for the next two weeks I did nothing but read Wolfe, right up to the poetic finale of his last book, *You Can't Go Home Again*.

138

Wearily, I returned to Professor Baker and wailed, "How can anyone ever be a writer? Thomas Wolfe has said it all!" In mock irritation, my white-haired professor replied, "Scott, come back to me when you're twenty-one."

While I was researching my subsequent biography of Perkins, I found a letter from someone who asked him whether Thomas Wolfe would always be read; and Perkins replied, "So long as there are sophomores in college."

So stretch a little, Snoopy. Your glib response suggests that Lucy's casting pearls before beagles. Why don't you part your dog-lips and try biting off a little more than you can chew? Join Lucy and me and thousands of other "sophomores" by discovering the inspiration in the works of Wolfe . . . and other daunting authors.

Winner of the Pulitzer Prize, **A. Scott Berg** *has written biographies of Maxwell Perkins, Samuel Goldwyn, Charles Lindbergh, and is currently writing the life of Woodrow Wilson.*

Wearily, I returned to Professor Baker and wailed, "How can anyone ever be a writer? Thomas Wolfe has said it all!"

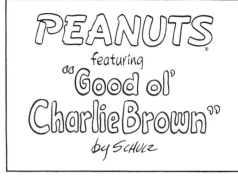

PEANUTS®
featuring
"Good ol' Charlie Brown"
by Schulz

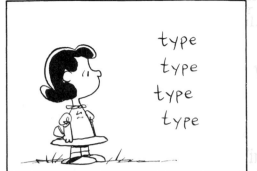

type
type
type
type

Toodle-oo, Caribou!
A Tale of the
Frozen North

The stall was empty!
"Someone has stolen my
polar cow!" shouted Joe Eskimo.

"This is the work
of Joe Jacket,
who hates me!"

MAY I SEE HOW
YOUR NEW NOVEL IS
COMING ALONG?

BE MY
GUEST..

10-15

"JOE ESKIMO AND JOE JACKET WERE RIVALS
FOR THE HEART OF SALLY SNOW WHO LIVED
SOUTH OF THE ICEBERG...JOE ESKIMO THOUGHT
BACK TO THE NIGHT HE FIRST SHOOK HER HAND"

"'I THINK YOU ARE
VERY NICE,' HE HAD
TOLD HER, AND THEY
SHOOK HANDS."

THEY
SHOOK
HANDS?

I THINK
YOUR LOVE
SCENE NEEDS
A LITTLE
SOMETHING..

I ALWAYS GET
SO EMBARRASSED..

139

Sol Stein

It would appear that the Eminent Beagle is having trouble writing love scenes; he should not treat them lightly if he wants his work to succeed.

Among the many advantages of a love scene is that it provides excellent opportunities for characterizing both partners and for creating sympathy or antipathy toward one of the characters.

Love stories exist about each of the seven ages of man. Three of those ages are most useful to the writer.

The youngest lovers may be inexperienced, tentative, nervous, worried about pregnancy, disease, getting caught. Any or all of these can become a writer's petri dish for brewing conflict and drama. External obstacles loom in abundance. The young lovers may be separated by distance because of school, work, family, and in Romeo's case, a balcony. They may have to overcome class differences, family incompatibilities, peer pressure, or rivalry from another young person, or from an older, more experienced individual. Keep in mind that you don't want to tell the reader what she is feeling, but to evoke feelings in the reader as a result of what the young lovers say to each other and what they do. It helps make each of them vulnerable in a different way.

With adult lovers in the child-bearing age group, one of the most powerful forces of nature is at work, the drive toward procreation, often unknown to or unacknowledged by lovers. The human race is perpetuated by drives that are endocrinal in origin. Romantic love, as it is experienced by most (but not all) people, is a cultural invention. While these are things that the average reader doesn't want to hear about, it is important that the writer know them. Love scenes deal with the consequences of these physiological drives and cultural customs. Writers need to be knowledgeable about the nuances of human relationships and the origins of feelings; hence, it helps for writers to know and understand as much as possible about the psychology and physiology underlying love—what the pulls are, whether or not the participants are aware of them.

An obstacle commonly faced by adult lovers is the threat of a competing person and the consequent loss of security in a relationship. An adult wandering from a relationship can get involved with persons of questionable character and can blunder into acts of violence. The consequences of infidelity have inspired hundreds of plots. Some obstacles encountered by adult lovers are internal, such as guilt over conduct disapproved of by the person or by society. Also casting a shadow over both old and new relationships is the fear of passing age boundaries, of getting older.

Keep in mind that you don't want to tell the reader what she is feeling, but to evoke feelings in the reader as a result of what the young lovers have to say to each other and what they do. It helps make each of them vulnerable in a different way.

In plotting a love story, a writer must remind himself that plot grows out of character. What happens in a love scene should come out of the writer's understanding of his characters and their motivation, and the clash between such characteristics or motivation in different characters.

The most boring kind of relationship is one in which there are never any problems. He loved her and she loved him, they never quarreled, is the ultimate turnoff. In devising a love story, search for the root conflicts based on character and upbringing, but also ferret out surface conflict by asking yourself if you have depicted your adult lovers at a moment of crisis. If not, can you add a crisis that will increase the tension of the relationship? Does the woman want something reasonable that is refused by the man, perhaps for reasons that he keeps secret and that arouse her suspicions? Does the man want something that is refused by the woman because she is afraid of the result? Whatever your plan, remember that if there is no friction between the lovers, there is no interest on the part of the reader. And if there is massive friction, will the reader be convinced that they are nevertheless in love? If they are not, you don't have a love story.

So, Snooper, old boy, it's back to the Olivetti—and give your lovers hell!

For years **Sol Stein** *was the editor of many famous writers. He himself has written nine novels, including* The Magician; Broadway plays; nonfiction books; screenplays; Stein on Writing; *and* How to Grow a Novel. *He is the creator of the computer software,* WritePro.™

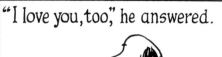

Ed McBain

You're on the right track, Snoops.

I never start a novel until I'm satisfied with the title. Generally, I'll know what the theme's going to be, and I'll know what kind of characters I'll need to keep the plot engine going, but I won't start a book until I have the title firmly in mind.

I don't believe in detailed outlines because once a book has been outlined too rigidly, the rest is only typing—and that's no fun. Instead, I'll search around for the right title, changing it, nudging it, polishing it, getting it to say exactly what I want it to say. Thanks to the magic of computers, I can try the title in different fonts and sizes, and I can print it in different colors. Once I feel I've got what I want, I drop those printed pages here and there around the office, face up, on desktop or filing cabinet, hither and yon, all over the place.

Then—whenever I'm in danger of losing track of the story or theme—I'll ask myself, "What's this book about?" And I'll look up from the machine, and there's the answer on all

those scattered pages, there's the *title!* One day, that title, gloriously rendered in foil on a magnificent book jacket, will tell the reader what the book is all about. But while I'm still working on the book, those pages with the title on them keep me focused and tell me where I'm going.

So, yes, Snoopy, m'lad, you are right to work on that title—*Dumb* or *Beyond Dumb* or even *From Dumb to Eternity*—until it tells you what your book is all about.

That ain't dumb at all, believe me.

 I don't believe in detailed outlines because once a book has been outlined too rigidly, the rest is only typing—and that's no fun.

Ed McBain, *who also writes as* **Evan Hunter,** *is the author of some ninety books, including* The Blackboard Jungle *and* Money, Money, Money.

her...   stormy knight.

It was a dark
   and stormy
Christmas night,

...eanwhile, on a sma...
...nsas, a boy was gr...

   End of Part I

...e climbed into
...carriage, he
...ed goodbye.

"How can I take you
anyplace when it's a
dark and stormy night?"
he said.

Call me
   Ishmael.

...uddenly, their dog, Rex,
...decided he'd better
...ke over!

...erent,"
...ll   It was a dark
              and stormy night

He also said,
...Have a nice day!"

     By Supper

...eir eyes met...   Possessed
...ve minutes later
...ey were married.

150

...s a crowded
...He was lonely.

"Our love is different," she cried. "It will endure forever."

AH! MY SECRETARY WITH THE MORNING MAIL...

Dear Contributor,
Thank you for submitting your manuscript. We regret that it does not suit our present needs.

ANOTHER REJECTION SLIP...

RATS!

OH, WELL, TAKE IT AND FILE IT WITH THE OTHERS...

7-4

Jack Canfield

Listen, Snoopy, you think you're the only one who has known rejection?

- Louis L'Amour, successful author of more than one hundred western novels with more than two hundred million copies in print, received 350 rejections before he made his first sale. He later became the first American novelist to receive a special congressional gold medal in recognition of his distinguished career as an author and contributor to the nation through his historically based books.

- Dr. Seuss's first children's book, *And to Think That I Saw It on Mulberry Street,* was rejected by twenty-seven publishers. The twenty-eighth publisher, Vanguard Press, sold six million copies of the book. All of Seuss's children's books went on to sell a total of more than one hundred million copies.

- Margaret Mitchell's classic *Gone With the Wind* was turned down by more than twenty-five publishers.

- Mary Higgins Clark was rejected forty times before selling her first story. More than thirty million copies of her books are now in print.

- Jack London received six hundred rejection slips before he sold his first story.

Eight years after his novel *Steps* won the National Book Award, Jerzy Kosinski permitted a writer to change his name and the title and send a manuscript of the novel to thirteen agents and fourteen publishers to test the plight of new writers. They all rejected it, including Random House, which had published it.

Novelist Carson McCullers endured three strokes before she was twenty-nine. While she was crippled, partially paralyzed, and in constant pain, she suffered the profound shock of her husband's suicide. Others may have surrendered to such afflictions, but she settled for writing no less than a page a day. On that unrelenting schedule, she turned out many distinguished novels, including *Member of the Wedding*, *The Ballad of the Sad Café* and *The Heart Is a Lonely Hunter*.

When we completed *Chicken Soup for the Soul*, it was turned down by thirty-three publishers in New York and another ninety at the American Booksellers Association convention in Anaheim, California, before Health Communications, Inc., finally agreed to publish it. All the major New York publishers said, "It is too nicey-nice" and "Nobody wants to read a book of short little stories." Since that time, more than eight million copies of the original book have been sold. The series, which has grown to thirty-two titles, in thirty-one languages, has sold more than fifty-three million copies.

So keep these failures and successes in mind, Snoopy—and go back to the Olivetti and give your story all you've got!

Jack Canfield's *amazing series,* Chicken Soup for the Soul, *is a publishing phenomenon, and* Chicken Soup for the Writer's Soul *is a must-read for every writer.*

Dear Editor,
    I am sending you
my latest novel.

8-8

HERE, THIS
JUST CAME
FOR YOU..

© 1994 United Feature Syndicate, Inc.

Don't!

Gentlemen,

12-10

© 1983 United Feature Syndicate, Inc.

Enclosed please find
the manuscript of
my new novel.

HERE,
YOU JUST
GOT A
LETTER

Dear Contributor,
    Already we
hate it.

Shelly Lowenkopf

There is something inherently satisfying in the way everyone's favorite beagle reacts to rejection slips. He brings the concept of the reptilian-brain response to new heights—beagle-brain heights.

I am comforted by the sight and thought of this particular strip because, after all these years of sending things forth (my first "big-time" acceptance letter was from the venerable *Amazing Stories* in 1953), rejection slips, particularly the generic ones that could have just as well been sent by the janitor as the editor, still rankle. *(I feel your pain, Snoopy.)*

Yes, I still get them, and yes, the sight of them still stings, but over the years I've learned something Snoopy hasn't.

The rejection slips I get now often invite me to resubmit, sometimes even going so far as to say when and, in some cases, suggesting a theme.

Rejection slips are living proof that I send my work forth, that I am being read, that I am casting my lot. They help define me to my writing self. When I settled into my preoccupation with

157

the literary short story, based in humor, irony, and sadly acquired wisdom, I had an amazing run of luck with the late great editor, John Milton, of the venerable *South Dakota Review*. We were quickly on a first name basis. He took everything I wrote and sent me a note saying, "I guess you're one of my regulars now." At which point he never took another story from me.

I kept sending my work out, using "ink," the handwritten encouragement on rejection slips, to cue me where to send the new material first.

Even as I write this, I'm still smarting from a rejecting letter sent by the editor of a literary magazine I'd tried for the first time. The editor thought my work more appropriate for sitcom television but certainly not for a literary magazine. I thought of Snoopy, who says, "Augh!" as well as it has ever been said. Even though I didn't agree with the contents of the letter, it was way up the scale from a form rejection slip; it was a carefully crafted personal letter.

I responded with a letter of thanks.

The point is simple enough: Don't let rejection slips or letters keep you from being the writer you want to be—the only writer you can be.

> *Rejection slips are living proof that I send my work forth, that I am being read, that I am casting my lot. They help define me to my writing self.*

Shelly Lowenkopf *has taught writing at the University of Southern California since 1974, in addition to having held major editorial positions with book publishers in the general trade, literary, mass market, and scholarly fields. The author of more than a dozen mass-market originals in fiction and another half dozen in nonfiction, he has served two terms as a regional president of the Mystery Writers of America.*

Ray Bradbury

The amazing Blackstone came to town when I was seven, and I saw how he came alive onstage and thought, *God, I want to grow up to be like that!* And I ran up to help him vanish an elephant. To this day I don't know where that elephant went. One moment it was there, the next—*abracadabra*—with a wave of the wand it was gone!

In 1929 Buck Rogers came into the world, and on that day in October a single panel of the Buck Rogers comic strip hurled me into the future. I never came back.

It was only natural when I was twelve that I decided to become a writer and laid out a huge roll of butcher paper to begin scribbling an endless tale that scrolled right on up to Now, never guessing that the butcher paper would run forever.

Snoopy has written me on many occasions from his miniature typewriter, asking me to explain what happened to me in the great blizzard of rejection slips of 1935. Then there was the snowstorm of rejection slips in '37 and '38 and an even worse winter snowstorm of rejections

…starting when I was fifteen I began to send short stories to magazines like Esquire, and they, very promptly, sent them back two days before they got them!

when I was twenty-one and twenty-two. That almost tells it, doesn't it, that starting when I was fifteen I began to send short stories to magazines like *Esquire*, and they, very promptly, sent them back two days before they got them! I have several walls in several rooms of my house covered with the snowstorm of rejections, but they didn't realize what a strong person I was; I persevered and wrote a thousand more dreadful short stories, which were rejected in turn. Then, during the late forties, I actually began to sell short stories and accomplished some sort of deliverance from snowstorms in my fourth decade. But even today, my latest books of short stories contain at least seven stories that were rejected by every magazine in the United States and also in Sweden! So, dear Snoopy, take heart from this. The blizzard doesn't last forever; it just seems so.

Ray Bradbury *is the author of dozens of books, including* The Martian Chronicles. *He has also written hundreds of short stories, poems, plays, and screenplays.*

163

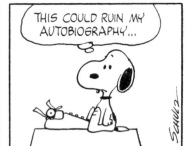

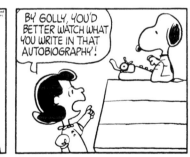

164

Charles Champlin

Snoopy had the right idea. Seated at his Olivetti portable typewriter balanced improbably on the top of a peaked roof, he launched an autobiography. No one else could tell the full story of the puppy farm or his later circle of friends. No one else knew it all, even his brother, Spike, stuck in the desert without a typewriter and only cacti to dictate to.

Doing an autobiography is more than an exercise in ego (although it is undoubtedly that, too); it is the capturing of a unique piece of history, a place, a time, and a portrait.

Anyone who aspires to write or who would simply like to tell children and grandchildren, "This is where you came from and this is what it was like when I was there," could begin by keeping a journal. We swear there are events in our lives we will never forget, yet our lives slip through our fingers like sand at the beach. As a test, one day set on paper not just what happened but what you thought about, worried about, observed, heard, even the public events that

165

stormy knight.

It was a dark
and storm
Christmas n

anwhile   farm in
nsas, a f   up.
    End of Part I

e climbed into
carriage, he
ed goodbye.

"How can I take you
Call me   anyplace when it's a
Ishmael.   dark and stormy night?"
               he said.

uddenly, their dog, Rex,
decided he'd better
ake over!

erent,"
ll   It was a dark
               and stormy night

He also said,
Have a nice day!"

By Supper
heir eyes met... Possessed
ive minutes later
ey were married.
166
s a crowded
He was lonely

 We swear there are events in our lives we will never forget, yet our lives slip through our fingers like sand at the beach.

might affect you sooner or later. Put the paper away. Look at it again in as little as two weeks' time, and be amazed how much has gone out of mind.

The autobiography is a summoning of memory, nothing so simple as "And then I worked for . . ." or "And then we moved to . . ." What color were your grandmother's eyes? What about the washcloths your great-uncle had sewn so he could clean both his ears at once? All those minor but revealing details are the flavorings of the slice of history only you as a writer can carve.

It is a gift to your family and your friends (now perhaps scattered over the country or the world). It may command no larger audience than that. But it may. Your slice of life becomes part of the mosaic of your times.

You need not be famous to write something worth remembering, worth preserving, worth publishing.

Charles Champlin's *books include a memoir,* Back There Where the Past Was, *about his boyhood in a small town in upstate New York. This famed critic's new book is* Back Where the Future Began.

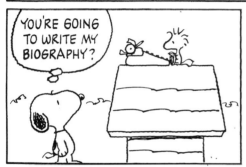

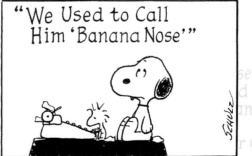

YOU KNOW WHAT'S A GOOD BOOK? "TREASURE ISLAND" BY ROBERT LOUIS STEVENSON...

IT'S VERY EXCITING... IF I WERE A WRITER, THAT'S THE KIND OF BOOK I'D WRITE

7-21 © 1964 United Feature Syndicate, Inc.

"Beagle Island"

"Jogging For Everyone"

9-28

A Detailed Guide to Running

Chapter One

The Left Foot

© 1978 United Feature Syndicate, Inc.

PEANUTS by Schulz

EDITORIAL QUEEN —

It was a dark and stormy night

Suddenly, a shot rang out.

LET ME SEE WHAT YOU'VE WRITTEN SO FAR..

YOU KNOW, WHEN YOU'RE WRITING A STORY, IT'S VERY IMPORTANT TO SELECT THE PERFECT WORDS...

IN THIS CASE, I WONDER IF "SUDDENLY" IS THE RIGHT WORD..

Gradually, a shot rang out.

10-24

Laird Koenig

Snoopy turns from his typewriter, reads a novel, sees a movie or a play. His interest slumps. He doesn't care what happens next. Why? The plot hasn't thickened. It's curdled. Not enough heat. The lead character lacks the fire to want something enough to make us root for him or her. When a plot works we feel what Scarlett, Oedipus, Captain Ahab, Frodo, and Bambi want more than anything else in the world.

Like all beginning writers, Snoopy is worried about plot. Whether thickening or thinning, there are some basic facts—I won't say rules—about plot that Snoopy should consider.

You don't even have to like Richard III or Lady Macbeth or Hannibal Lecter as long as you feel their drive and understand what it is they absolutely must do. Put your character in jail. He wants out. In a hospital? She wants to live and prays the donor's transplant arrives on time. In war? Our hero splashes in blood to survive. In love? Ah, in love. Two hearts will break if they can't reach each other's arms. Caution, Snoopy. The love story may be the most difficult plot to

handle. How do you keep the lovers apart and panting for most of the story? *Romeo and Juliet* works because they had big in-law troubles and a very high balcony; the most important part of that scene *is* the balcony.

Snoopy's beginning to suspect plotting like this sounds like the classic setup for a thriller. Too formulaic? Too simple? Not for Shakespeare. Not when the ghost of Hamlet's father lays it on him to avenge his murder. Suddenly this overly intellectual prince must pick up a sword. Before this character can kill his uncle he keeps us spellbound step by step facing life and death before time runs out. Good enough for our fellow writer, Shakespeare, Snoopy.

 When a plot works we feel what Scarlett, Oedipus, Captain Ahab, Frodo, and Bambi want more than anything else in the world.

Granted that besides a driving plot there are other ways to hold a reader or an audience, but can you pull off the conjuring act of a Marcel Proust? For most of us, take another look at what you've written. Are we living the heartbeat, love, terror of characters we understand and know what they want more than anything in life and must do in their race against time?

So, Snooper old boy, if you just can find out what your characters want, your plot will take care of itself. And remember—stories aren't written—they're rewritten.

Laird Koenig *has written seven plays and six novels and has the distinction of having written Jodie Foster's first starring film,* The Little Girl Who Lived Down the Lane, *as well as Sir Laurence Olivier's next-to-last one,* Inchon.

172

...lonely.   He was a dark and
her...   stormy knight.

It was a dark
   and stormy
Christmas night.

...eanwhile, on a small farm in
...nsas, a boy was growing up.
   End of Part I

...he climbed into
...carriage, he
...ved goodbye.

"How can I take you
  anyplace when it's a
  dark and stormy night?"
        he said.

Call me
  Ishmael.

...uddenly, their dog, Rex,
...decided he'd better
...ake over!

...ferent,"
...ill   It was a dark
                and stormy night

...He also said,
..."Have a nice day!"

        By Supper
...heir eyes met... Possessed
...ive minutes later
...hey were married.

...as a crowded

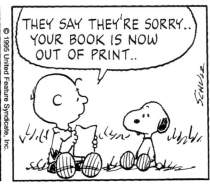

Cooking Hints

When mixing dog food in a bowl, the water can either be put in first or added last.

Who cares?

11-14

© 1989 United Feature Syndicate, Inc.

Julia Child

Snoopy, if you do want to write a cookbook, I hope you'll go at it with all four feet and produce the first book of really fine gourmet food for dogs, good enough for humans, too.

I think the first requirement is that you get yourself the best possible training. I always recommend one of the fine culinary schools, especially the Culinary Institute of America in New York. Although on-the-job training is good, you will rarely get the whole of the vast culinary vocabulary except at an accredited professional school. It probably doesn't take dogs per se, but attach yourself to one of the students and just stick with him or her at all times. Good training gives you confidence—you know what you are doing, and you've learned it the right way.

Then, initial training under your belt, you want to work with the finest chefs in the business, and you start at the bottom—no matter how much you paid for your schooling! You must know every aspect of the kitchen from the lowest position to that of master chef. Thus, you pick up the right work habits, and this takes time—a good year or more. When you've mastered one

...you pick up the right work
habits, and this takes time —
a good year or more.

restaurant, pick another to enlarge your experiences. You need to count on at least ten years of hard work to get yourself the proper background before you can consider yourself a fully qualified chef. The great thing about this profession is that you have entered a big international family of enthusiastic people who love their work, and with few exceptions, love each other.

And now you are ready to write your book! It will be unique. I don't think any publisher will be able to keep his paws off it, and both the canine and the rest of the public will eat it up. Good luck, Snoopy, and get moving!

Julia Child *has written dozens of books since the start of her show,* The French Chef, *and her first book,* Mastering the Art of French Cooking. *She is one of the most famous chefs in America.*

176

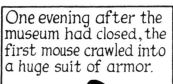

PEANUTS — Though her husband often went on business trips, she hated to be left alone.

"I've solved our problem," he said. "I've bought you a St. Bernard. It's name is Great Reluctance."

"Now, when I go away, you shall know that I am leaving you with Great Reluctance!"

She hit him with a waffle iron.

PEANUTS — His wife had always hated his work.

"You'll never make any money growing toadstools," she complained.

"On the contrary," he declared. "My toadstool business is mushrooming!"

She creamed him with the electric toaster.

PEANUTS

They had named their Great Dane "Good Authority."

12-10

One day, she asked her husband if he had seen her new belt.

"Belt?" he said. "Oh, I'm sorry. I thought it was a dog collar. I have it on Good Authority."

Shortly thereafter, their marriage began to go downhill.

SCHULZ

Elmore Leonard

Snoopy has come up with an especially clever name with "Good Authority," one that makes the story work.

I once named a character Frank Matisse, but he acted older than his age; and for some reason he wouldn't talk as much as I wanted him to. I changed his name to Jack Delany and couldn't shut him up.

Because I use a lot of dialogue in my stories, the characters must be able to talk in interesting ways. So I audition them in opening scenes to see which ones will have important roles in the plot. If a character doesn't speak the way I want him to, and changing his name doesn't work, he could be demoted to a less important role.

The best kind of character is one who starts out in a minor role—sometimes without even having a name—and talks his way into the plot. He says a few words, and I see this guy has an interesting personality, and I look for more ways to use him in the story.

I write my stories in scenes and always from a particular character's point of view. Then I may rewrite the same scene from a different character's point of view and find that it works better. After I finish a book, I continue to think about my characters and wonder what they're up to.

The most important advice I would suggest to beginning writers: Try to leave out the parts that readers skip.

 The best kind of character is one who starts out in a minor role—sometimes without even having a name—and talks his way into the plot.

Elmore Leonard *is the best-selling author of more than thirty books, including* Get Shorty, La Brava, Cuba Libre, *and* Stick, *most of which have been made into films.*

180

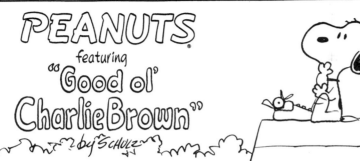

The last car drove away. It began to rain.

And so our hero's life ended as it had begun... a disaster.

"I never got any breaks," he had always complained.

He had wanted to be rich. He died poor. He wanted friends. He died friendless.

He wanted to be loved. He died unloved. He wanted laughter. He found only tears.

He wanted applause. He received boos. He wanted fame. He found only obscurity. He wanted answers. He found only questions.

I'M HAVING A HARD TIME ENDING THIS..

SOMETIMES, WHEN YOU ARE A GREAT WRITER, THE WORDS COME SO FAST YOU CAN HARDLY PUT THEM DOWN ON PAPER...

SOMETIMES

J.F. Freedman

And when the words don't come at all, as Snoopy is experiencing in panels three and four, or leak out in tiny, unsatisfactory dribs and drabs, then you've entered the arena in which the actual process of honest-to-God writing, on a steady, daily basis, takes place. What Snoopy is experiencing in panel two, the unconscious flow of ideas that come out of the ends of the fingers onto the page, is more akin to catching lightning in a bottle—you hold up the bottle and miraculously, there's the light. All that was necessary for you to do was to be there and have a proper receptacle to hold the lightning—the idea—in. It's an unconscious process, not that dissimilar from breathing or belching, but more enjoyable, because when you're done you have something tangible and permanent. It may be imperfect when seen in the next day's light; it may need a lot of revision, but it's there.

Usually, meaning 95 percent of the time (that's conservative), it doesn't happen like that. Yes, you have an understanding of the themes, who the characters are, what the plot points should be—you'd better, or you shouldn't be writing this particular story in the first place. But putting those elements together in the best (and ultimately only) sequence, when it isn't coming effortlessly, as it is when you're in that unconscious state of bliss, is where the real writing takes place. It's about sitting your butt down and making something happen. That something can be anything. It doesn't have to be directly tied into the story line or characters or themes you're with at that particular moment in your book, or even be about anything that particular book is trying to say at all. The important thing is to write, to commit words to paper, whether you're using ballpoint pen and legal pad, typewriter, computer, or whatever medium you fancy.

When I find myself in Snoopy's position in panel four, I often step back and come at my work sideways. I'll write a sketch of one of my characters or a descriptive passage relating to, but not usually in direct linear relationship with, my story. Sometimes I won't write on my story at all. I'll write about something else. It could be an entry in my journal, a paragraph or more about another idea that's been rolling around in the back of my mind, a letter to one of my kids at college, whatever. The important thing is to keep the machine lubricated and running. What happens, generally, is that once you do sit down and start on something, it becomes easy to get back into the flow of what your primary writing mission is, and the blank sheet of paper or blank computer screen becomes alive again.

Like almost all professional writers I know, I approach writing as a job, something I have to do every day (weekends and holidays excepted, like any other job). It happens to be the best job I know of, because you're in complete control and you're actually creating something out of nothing. I have had an office away from my home for almost twenty years, and I'm usually there

It was a dark
and stormy
Christmas night.

End of Part I

meanwhile...farm in
...sas, ...up.

climbed into
carriage, he
d goodbye.

"How can I take you
anyplace when it's a
dark and stormy night?"
he said.

Call me
Ishmael.

ddenly, their dog, Rex,
ecided he'd better
ke over!

ent,"

It was a dark
and stormy night

He also said,
lave a nice day!"

By Supper
ir eyes met... Possessed
e minutes later
y were married.

a crowded
le was lonely.

stormy knight.

For me as a writer, and I think
this is true of most writers, characters
are what a story is about—they drive the story;
plot and theme come from character, not the
other way around. The writer is along for
the ride and to give direction …

from nine or ten in the morning until at least three in the afternoon; usually, it's more like five or six. I don't have set hours—write from ten until one, lunch from one until two-thirty, write from three to six, for instance—but I make sure I'm writing something every day. When things are going well, I usually rewrite the previous day's work in the morning when I start up and then go on to new material. I like to get the casual, nonwriting stuff—the newspaper reading and coffee-drinking—out of the way before I begin, and then I try to work with a minimum of distraction. When I'm into a project, after the initial false starts and stops, whether it's a novel, short story, or screenplay, I insist on getting a certain amount of work done before packing it up for the day—usually a minimum of three pages, which to me is about twelve hundred words, but with any determination and luck, it's more like five to eight pages.

For me as a writer, and I think this is true of most writers, characters are what a story is about—they drive the story; plot and theme come from character, not the other way around. The writer is along for the ride and to give direction, like a stagecoach driver pulling on the reins. The horses, your characters, are doing the work. You're making sure they don't run off a cliff.

One last word about Snoopy, *Peanuts*, and comics in general. I feel strongly that they're some of the best writing we have. Until I was in junior high school, all I read were comic books and comic strips. Great comic strips, from *Krazy Kat* through *Peanuts* to *The Far Side* and *Calvin and Hobbes*, are a fine introduction into literature, and are damn good writing in and of themselves. They have to be enjoyable, they have to be honest—you can't hide in a comic strip—they have to have continuity, which they achieve through the singular talent and point of view of their creator, and at the same time each strip has to stand alone and work in its own right, without support from those that came before it or will come after it. If we're trying to promote literacy and enjoyment of reading in our young generations, distributing comic strips and comic books in our schools might be one of the best ways to get students' heads out of video games and television sets and into literature.

 Once a film director, **J.F. Freedman** *has an amazing string of suspenseful best-sellers:* The Obstacle Course, House of Smoke, Against the Wind, Key Witness, The Disappearance, Above the Law, *and his latest,* Bird's-Eye View.

About the Editors

O. Henry Prize short story winner **Barnaby Conrad** *has authored thirty books, including* Matador, Hemingway's Spain, The Complete Guide to Writing Fiction, *and* Name Dropping, *the story of his San Francisco saloon. He wrote a* Playhouse 90 *for John Frankenheimer, the screenplay for John Steinbeck's* Flight, *and a Broadway play based on his novel* Dangerfield.

Monte Schulz *is the son of Charles M. Schulz. He has a master's degree in American Studies from the University of California at Santa Barbara and is the author of the novel* Down By The River. *He divides his time between Nevada City, California, and Santa Barbara, where he is finishing his second novel.*